THE POCKET
DARING BOOK FOR GIRLS:
THINGS TO DO

PRAISE FOR *THE DARING BOOK FOR GIRLS*

"An old-fashioned-fun-and survival guide specifically for the pigtail pack . . . offers primers on everything from changing a tire and negotiating pay to basic karate moves and lighthearted pranks. Now Hayley has no excuse for sitting at the computer while Zack is up in his tree house."—*Reader's Digest*

"With tips on doing cartwheels and pulling pranks, *The Daring Book for Girls* is old-school cool—like its bestselling brother *The Dangerous Book for Boys.*"—*Good Housekeeping*

"The authors mix inspiring tales of girls who made good . . . with a scrap bag of how-tos for girlish activities . . . *The Daring Book for Girls* keeps . . . practical knowledge from getting drowned in the techno-flow."—*The New York Times*

"The essential how-to manual for the modern-day girl."—*Teen Vogue*

"Not that we're feeling competitive, but *The Dangerous Book for Boys* does seem a wee bit . . . exclusionary. Happily, *The Daring Book for Girls* shows the women of the future—and their adventurous elders (us!)—everything from how to tie a sari to how to negotiate a salary and clues them in on the first rules of softball (never apologize unless you actually bop someone). Among the joys: nearly extinct games (like "Light as a Feather, Stiff as a Board") that may have eluded you while you were busy with Barbie and boy toys."—*O, The Oprah Magazine*

THE POCKET DARING BOOK FOR GIRLS: THINGS TO DO

This book is a mix of much-loved chapters from the popular *The Daring Book for Girls,* plus new adventures and activities for readers to discover—all of which are perfect for the rambling days of summer, or any season. With its fun, portable size and compelling contents, this book of Things To Do is perfect for any girl on the go.

Daring Girl badges and other downloads available at
www.daringbookforgirls.com

THE POCKET DARING BOOK FOR GIRLS: THINGS TO DO

HarperCollins books may be purchased for educational, business,
or sales promotional use. For information, please write:
Special Markets Department, HarperCollins Publishers,
10 East 53rd Street, New York, NY 10022.

FIRST EDITION

NOTE TO PARENTS: This book contains a number of activities which may be dangerous if not done exactly as directed or which may be inappropriate for young children. All of these activities should be carried out under adult supervision only. The authors and publishers expressly disclaim liability for any injury or damages that result from engaging in the activities contained in this book.

Illustrations by Alexis Seabrook

Designed by Richard J. Berenson, Berenson Design & Books, LLC and The Stonesong Press, LLC

Library of Congress Cataloging-in-Publication Data has been applied for.

ISBN: 978-0-06-167307-8

08 09 10 11 12 ❖/RRD 10 9 8 7 6 5 4 3 2 1

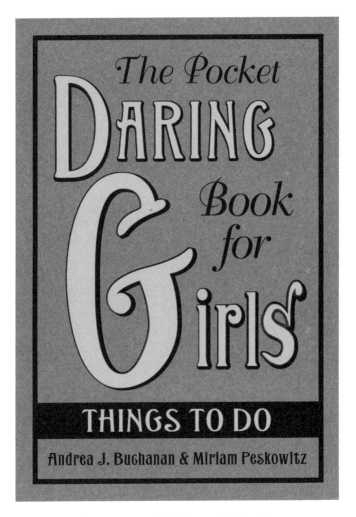

The Pocket
DARING
Book
for
Girls

THINGS TO DO

Andrea J. Buchanan & Miriam Peskowitz

Illustrations by Alexis Seabrook

Collins

An Imprint of HarperCollinsPublishers

Contents

CONTENTS

Introduction

We love books. Fancy books, heavy books, books with gilded pages—you name it. But fancy books, impressive as they may be, aren't always practical to read on the go. This pocket book—small enough to fit in a backpack or beachbag—lends itself much better to adventuring. So we took our favorite outdoor and rainy-day activities from the original *The Daring Book for Girls* and assembled them into this pint-sized edition of Things to Do. Plus we added lots of new chapters we just know girls (and probably some boys, too) will love—wait until you read about making a zip line and skateboarding!

We hope you enjoy this collection of old and new favorites as you celebrate the Daring Girl credo: Enjoy yourself. Explore new things. Lead an interesting life.

Bon Voyage!

Andrea J. Buchanan
Miriam Peskowitz

Sleep Outs

A quick backyard tent can be made with just a rope, some stakes, and two tarps—big plastic, waterproof sheets essential to camping. First, string a rope between two branches on two different trees. Then stretch one tarp out on the ground and hang the second over the rope. Lastly, stake the four corners of the hanging tarp to the ground, using a hammer or a rock.

Store-bought tents are much larger than ever before, and come with flexible poles that fold into foot-long lengths and stow away in a nylon sack, making tent-pitching relatively simple. They also better protect us from the number one evil scourge of camping: bugs. (The number two evil scourge, should you ask, is poison ivy.) This leads to the prime rule of tents: Keep the zipper shut, because it's nearly impossible to shoo a mosquito out of your tent once it's in.

Before you pitch your tent, you may want to lay down an extra tarp to keep things extra clean and dry. (If you do, tuck the edges under so the tarp is slightly smaller than your tent.) Then set out the tent, and follow directions for inserting the poles. The fly, which protects from rain and dew, goes over the top of the tent and usually clips on, is staked to the ground, or both. Finally, bang the tent pegs into the ground, lest large gusts of wind send your tent soaring toward Kansas.

You've just made your home outdoors. Here are the basic furnishings:

♦ **The sleeping bag.** To make things a bit more comfortable, add a sleeping pad underneath and bring along a pillow or just a pillow case you can stuff with clothes. Sleeping pads have gotten softer, longer, and more elaborate, and can even involve air pumps, which your parents will undoubtedly appreciate if you invite them to sleep out with you.

If you don't have a sleeping bag, a jellyroll does the trick. (That's when you roll your sheet and blanket together inside your pillowcase, and sling it over your shoulder for the journey to your tent.)

◆ **Flashlight and bug spray.** Enough said.

◆ **A cooler.** Filled with lots of drinking water and camping food staples like fresh apples, dried fruit, trail mix, and beef jerky. Marshmallows are a necessity, too, if a campfire's involved, as are the other ingredients for s'mores: chocolate bars and graham crackers.

The anti-litter mantra for sleeping and camping outdoors is: take it in, take it out. Since there are no garbage cans in the wilderness, bring a bag for your wrappers and other trash.

Once you've learned to pitch a tent and roll out the sleeping bag in your backyard, you can graduate to the full-out camping experience, where the refrigerator and indoor toilet are not close at hand.

Camping is gear-intensive and takes careful planning,

especially if you're hiking a few miles out. You must carry in several days' food and water in your backpack, not to mention a camping stove and mess kit, soap and a toothbrush, and so much more. When you're ready for a first experience at a wilderness campground, find a friend whose family are pros, and learn from them.

Whether you are in your backyard or the Rocky Mountains, remember the whole point of sleeping out is to breathe in the night air, listen to nature's songs, and drift off to sleep under the stars.

⨞

Make Your Own Zip Line

If you can't globe-trot to Costa Rica and ride a zip line in full harness above the rainforest canopy, you can build a more modest zip line in your own backyard. Ours is simpler than a high-pressure steel cable stretched 400 feet high in the air, and uses a make-your-own grab bar and easily available rope.

You will need:

- ❖ Twelve metal coat hangers (more if they're thin)
- ❖ Wide electrical tape and duct tape
- ❖ Lots of polyethylene rope (aka clothesline)
- ❖ Pulley, sized to match the rope, and strong enough to hold your weight
- ❖ Tape measure

Optional

- ❖ One or two eyebolts, with nuts and washers
- ❖ Enough wooden planks (about 2″ x 10″) to make a ladder up your tree, a hammer and galvanized nails.

Building a zip line in your backyard presents a series of challenges to solve.

1. Where shall the zip line start and stop?

Find a jumping-off spot and a landing spot: two trees, a tree house, a swing set, a playscape with a ladder to a fort at the top, the edge of an elevated patio or deck. You can jump from the roof of a shed, or a banister off the second floor porch, or a tree in your neighbor's yard. Consider how tall you and your friends are, how high up in the air you want to be, and for how long. The zip line's starting point must be higher than the finishing point. Consider, too, the length of your line: too short and it's too quick a ride, but too long and it grinds to a stop, leaving you suspended in midair.

2. How will you climb to the starting point?

If the starting point is a tree, does it have low branches to climb? If not, find a ladder and wrap it against the tree, or hammer some wood planks into the trunk for footing. Galvanized nails are key because they won't rust and weaken.

3. How will you connect the rope to your starting point?

Once you've found your start and finish, measure the distance between them and triple or quadruple the number, since you'll need to wrap the line many times around the tree and tie it with a solid knot, and it's much easier to cut off extra rope than to discover you don't have enough. Wrap the rope five or six times around the tree at the height you've chosen. End with a tautline hitch—see the chapter on Knots and Stitches. Double it if you want to be extra sure.

However, according to our arborists, it's not so great to permanently wrap ropes around trees because it scars the bark and cuts off circulation. Believe it or not, it's better to knock a nail or bolt through a tree. For this option, find an eyebolt large enough for the rope and matched to the width of the tree, drill a large enough hole, and secure it with a nut, washers on both sides. Knot the rope to the bolt.

4. What's the best grab bar to use?

The grab bar needs to be secure enough that it won't disintegrate when you're holding on for dear life, and soft enough to hold comfortably with your hands as you whir through the air. Take your twelve metal hangers and undo the twist at the top of each one. Braid or weave the hangers together as best you can, to form a thick metal rope. Wrap the braided metal with several layers of electrical wire but leave a few inches at each end unwrapped. The bottom of the pulley has an opening for an attachment. Insert one end of the grab bar through this hole. Then sculpt the hangers into a circular or oval shape, and twist the strands together, one-to-one, to hold the circle tight. Wrap the whole contraption with electrical tape, and then wrap it again. After that, cover many times with duct tape. The more tape, the better.

Now thread the zip line rope—already attached to the jumping off spot—through the pulley. Cut a smaller piece of rope that you can use to pull the grab bar back to the starting point, and attach it to the grab bar. (By the way, once this system is up, you'll find many creative uses for pulleys. For instance, you might string a pulley system between your house and your friend's house next door and use clothespins or a basket to send messages, books, trading cards, and borrowed clothing back and forth. The possibilities are endless.)

5. What is the slope, and where is the endpoint.

The steeper the slope between the two trees, the faster the zip line will go and the more thrilling it will be. Leave enough give in the rope so the ride slows about three fourths of the way down. This will prevent you from slamming into a tree and wasting precious zip line time in the Emergency Room. (Some kids drag an old mattress against the landing point to cushion the ending.) A three-to-five foot difference in elevation between start and finish usually does the trick. Pull the rope tight at the ending point, wrap it many times around the tree, and make a tautline hitch (or use an eyebolt here, too). You may have to experiment a few times with how high you tie the rope, rewrapping and tying several times until, by trial and error, the perfect amount of tension and slope is found.

⌒⌒

Fourteen Games of Tag

A game of tag can be as basic or as complicated as you like: you can revel in the pure straightforwardness of one person chasing another, or liven things up by adding rules and strategy. Either way, tag requires no equipment, no court, no uniform—just someone willing to be It, and others willing to run as fast as it takes to avoid getting tagged and becoming It themselves. Here are fourteen ways of playing tag.

1. Blob Tag/Chinese Dragon Tag

In Blob Tag or Chinese Dragon Tag (also known as "chain tag," "amoeba tag," and "manhunt"), one person is It. But instead of being able to tag someone and no longer be It, the person who is It tags a player, and each player who is tagged then has to link arms with the tagger and join in as It. As more players are tagged, the link of taggers grows, making it look like a blob of people, or a Chinese dragon (hence the name). No tags count if the Blob separates. The game is over when the last player is finally tagged.

2. Freeze Tag

When a player is tagged in Freeze Tag, she must freeze in place immediately. Sometimes the game is played with the rule that other untagged players can unfreeze anyone who is frozen; the game can also be played so that the person who is It only wins when every single player is frozen.

3. Tornado Tag

Also called Hurricane Tag, Hurricane, and plain old Tornado, this variation of tag requires the person who is It to spin around like a tornado, with arms outstretched. If the person who is It tags someone without spinning, it doesn't count.

4. TV Tag

In this version of tag, your generally useless TV knowledge comes in handy by saving you from becoming It. When a player is about to be tagged by the person who is It, she can keep herself safe by touching the ground and shouting out the name of a TV show. If a player can't think of a show title before being tagged, or if she says a title someone else has already used, that player becomes It. (Another variation is to use movie titles or book titles.)

5. Shadow Tag

This game is perfect toward the end of a sunny day when shadows are long, since the main rule of Shadow Tag is that whoever is It can tag a player by stepping on her shadow.

6. Time Warp Tag

This kind of tag is played just like regular tag, except that at any point during the game play, any player (including whoever is It) can call out, "Time Warp!" whereupon all players must move in slow motion. When "Time Warp!" is called again, play returns to normal speed.

7. Line Tag

In Line Tag, which is played best on a playground or other surface with lines or painted areas on it, players are allowed to run or walk only on the lines. These can be hopscotch lines, basketball court lines, or even lines on the sidewalk—if it's a line, you can step on it. Otherwise, you're out. If a player is tagged, she must sit down, and the only player who can move past her is the one who is It.

8. Zombie Tag

The person who is It must chase after the players "zombie-style," staggering with her arms out in front of her and groaning like the undead. When the It zombie tags a player, that player also becomes a zombie. The game ends when all players have been transformed into moaning zombies.

9. Electric Tag

When a player is tagged (complete with electric-sounding "bzzt!" noises by person who is It), she must sit on the ground and become "electrified," which means that although she cannot stand up or move from her spot, she has the power of being It. The players who are not It and who have not been tagged must avoid being tagged by It and running too close to the electrified players, who are allowed to reach out and touch any player running past. Getting tagged by It or an electrified player means sitting down on the ground and becoming electrified yourself. The game continues until there is only one untagged, unelectrified player left.

10. Battle Tag

In this game, there are two players who are It: the Freezer, and the Heater. Everyone else is a Runner. The Freezer and Heater battle for control of the Runners—the Freezer wants everyone to be frozen, while the Heater wants everyone to be unfrozen. The Freezer freezes other players as in Freeze Tag, and the Heater unfreezes frozen players. The Heater cannot be frozen by the Freezer, and the Freezer cannot be melted by the Heater. The Freezer wins when all players are frozen before the Heater can get to them; the Heater wins when all players are unfrozen before the Freezer can refreeze them; the game is over when everyone is too tired to run anymore.

11. Inverted Tag

For Inverted Tag, everything is backward. There is only one player who is Not It, everyone else is It, and the object of the game is for everyone to chase the player who is Not It and tag her. Whoever stays Not It the longest is the winner.

12. Infection Tag

In Infection Tag, the player who is It infects everyone she tags, making every tagged player become It too. The last player tagged by any of the Its becomes the first It for the next round of infection.

13. Hot Lava Monster Tag

This version of tag is similar to the game of "hot lava," where certain areas of the ground are deemed hot lava, making them untouchable. In Hot Lava Monster Tag, which is best played on a playground, the entire ground is hot lava, and the "hot lava monster" (the person who is It) is the only person who can stand on it. Everyone else must move around on the play structures, being careful not to touch the ground. Any player who touches the ground or gets tagged by the hot lava monster becomes the new hot lava monster.

14. Hide and Seek Tag

This is best played in woods with lots of places to hide. Everyone who is not It runs off while the Seeker closes her eyes and counts to 100 next to a designated tree. The Seeker calls "Ready or Not, Here I Come," and begins searching for everyone else. The goal for those hiding is to get back to touch the tree before being tagged. Those who are tagged before touching the tree are also It and join the Seeker. The last one to reach the tree or be tagged is the Seeker in the next game.

❧

How to Run Faster

Ever felt like the slowest runner in the group? Running faster is a combination of finding a longer stride in your steps; adding more strides per minute; gaining muscle strength in your legs, arms, and torso; and visualizing yourself moving faster through the air. Here are things you can practice so you can run like the wind, or at least fast enough to stay in the game!

Push off from the ball and toes of your back foot. Really jettison your body forward and into the air. You'll feel the difference.

Lengthen your stride so your front leg extends to its full reach. If you aren't already leaning forward just a little bit as you run, try that. To get a sense of how this should feel, find a hill and run down, as the hill automatically lengthens your stride.

Pump your arms, forward and backward, "from pocket to jaw," as the coaches say, with your elbows at a ninety-degree angle. The hands and arms should point in the direction you are headed, which means your arms should neither cross in front of your body, nor flail out to the side. Relax your hands (no fists) and imagine holding a thin piece of paper between your thumb and third finger. Oh, and don't twist your chest and shoulders from side to side—only the arms move.

Try some interval training: jog for two minutes, sprint for thirty seconds, jog, sprint, jog, sprint. Or, near the end of a run, push yourself into a sprint. The sprint gets your body used to the extra effort of moving your legs faster, and eventually, running faster will feel normal.

Pretend that you are quickstepping your way across a field of hot coals. Or run up a flight of stairs (but walk down). Both exercises get you used to lifting your feet off the ground quickly.

Time yourself, then try to beat your last time. Some adults use running logs to keep a record of how far and fast they run, to see evidence that they are getting faster. Be kind to yourself, though. It's just running.

∽

Bandana Tying

The word *bandana* has a global history. It comes from the Sanskrit *bhandhana,* which means tying. The word was absorbed first into Portuguese (in the sixteenth century, Portugal had conquered the cities of Goa and Bombay, now called Mumbai, on the western coast of India). From Portuguese, the word entered English. We can thank Indian languages for an assortment of English clothing words, such as cashmere (from the north-

ern region of Kashmir), cummerbund, bangle, khaki, pajama, and dungaree.

Bandanas are often sold under the nondescript name "All Purpose Cloth," or APC. A bit of a boring moniker, perhaps, but, oh, so true. A bandana can be a belt, or a blindfold for Blind Man's Bluff. With a needle and thread, two or more can be sewn together to make a shirt or skirt.

You can wrap it loosely around your neck, cowboy style, pull it up over your nose and mouth for a disguise, or use it to dress up your pet. Best of all, you can wrap found treasures or lunch in an APC, then attach it to a long stick and sling it over your shoulder when you head out to see the world.

Bandanas are an excellent way to cover your hair, too, while playing lacrosse or hiking on a hot day, and they make perfect headbands.

To tie a bandana around your head, fold it in half to make a triangle. Place the long edge on your forehead, however low or high you want (you'll likely experiment with this, and try different possibilities). The cloth will fall lightly over your hair. With your hands, smooth it toward the back, push the tip of the triangle toward the

nape of your neck. Then draw the ends over it, and tie (use the square knot as described on page X).

You'll probably want to pull the triangle portion of the bandana into place, so it's smooth against your head, and so the corners don't stick out the sides.

If your head is larger, or if you want to make one for your mom or dad, instead of folding the cloth in half, merely fold one corner toward the opposite corner, and go from there.

To turn a bandana into a headband, fold in half to make a triangle. Start folding in, from the tip of the triangle toward the long edge, until you're left with the size headband you want to wear. Wrap around your head and tie in the back.

Building a Campfire

Sitting around a campfire is probably one of the oldest human activities. Nowadays, unless you're on a solo wilderness hike, a campfire is less a tool of survival than a social event—a chance to sing songs and tell stories and be out in the dark in nature with friends.

A fire needs three things: fuel, heat, and air. The most common fuel is wood—main fuel such as logs cut from trees, and smaller fuel like tinder (twigs, strips of paper, or anything small that burns well) and kindling (branches and twigs about the size of a pencil and no thicker than a finger). Heat, which comes in the form of a flame or

spark generated from matches, lighters, friction, or even focused sunlight, should be generated from the smaller fuel, which will then ignite the larger fuel. And of course, fire needs oxygen, so make sure that your fuel is packed loosely enough to allow for air circulation. When there's not enough oxygen present, the fire goes out, which is why dousing flames with water or smothering a small fire with sand extinguishes the flames.

What you'll need to build your own campfire:

- A fire ring, a fire pit, a fire pan, or other temporary fire site
- Water or sand to extinguish the fire
- Tinder
- Kindling
- Main fuel (thick, dry wood and logs—the thicker the wood, the longer the fire will burn)
- Matches or a lighter

BUILDING THE FIRE

The first item of business when building a fire is deciding where to make it. Find a spot away from tents, trees with low-hanging branches, or other flammable elements. Once you've determined your location, you can begin to assemble your fire. Ideally, you can use an existing fire pit or fire ring. If there isn't one handy, you can create a fire site yourself. One way is to clear away a space on the ground, dig a pit, line it with small rocks, and then cover that area about half an inch deep with sand or aluminum foil. Otherwise you can use a fire pan, either a store-bought metal pan for the purpose of making fires, or any round metal surface, such as a pizza pan or a trash can lid.

Once you have your site established, place your tinder (the small pieces you collected) in a small pile in the middle of the fire site. Around that, place the kindling, taking care not to pack it too tightly, as your fire will need air in order to burn. Arrange the kindling in a kind of "teepee" format, as though you are creating a small tent around your tinder. Leave an opening so that you can light the tinder, and keep some of your kindling in reserve, so you can add more to the fire as it takes hold.

Using a match, lighter, or your preferred method of ignition, light the tinder and gently fan or blow on it until it becomes a strong flame and ignites the kindling around it. Once the kindling is burning, you can add your main fuel—those large, thick logs that will burn long and bright. Add more kindling to the fire to keep the fire burning, but take care to keep the fire manageable. Also make sure to place your wood carefully, and not just throw it onto the fire.

Once the fire is dwindling and it's time to put it out, use water to douse the flames completely. You can also use sand, if that is available, to smother the fire. Water is the most thorough method of putting out a fire, and when it comes to extinguishing fires, you definitely want to be thorough. Check to make sure there's nothing still smoldering, even when it seems like the fire is out. Everything—the fire site, the burned fuel, the area around the fire—should be cool to the touch before you leave. A fire that is carelessly put out, or not put out thoroughly enough, can flare up again.

WHAT TO DO AROUND THE FIRE

If you have some long sticks or branches handy, and a bag full of marshmallows or a pack of hotdogs, you can use them to cook over the open fire. Skewer a marshmallow and hold it over the flames to toast it—if you have some handy, graham crackers and a chocolate bar can turn toasty marshmallows into delicious s'mores. Or break out the hotdogs and buns, spear a dog with your branch, and roast it to perfection. A campfire is also the perfect setting for singing songs and telling ghost stories.

PRECAUTIONS AND TIPS

- Check with the local firehouse or Park Ranger to see if campfires are permitted. Often you will need a permit to make any type of open fire outside—even in your own backyard.

- Clear the fire site before you start and after you're done. You don't want to leave a mess behind—or anything that could potentially start another fire.

- Never use flammable liquid or aerosols on a fire.

- Build your campfire far enough from your tent and other trees and low-hanging branches so that stray sparks won't start a fire outside the pit.

- Do not build your fire on peat or grass.

- Don't pick up burning wood.

- Wind can spread fire quickly, so make sure to build your fire in a place shielded from gusts.

Making a Cloth-Covered Book

You will need:

- ❖ Two pieces of $6^{1}/_{2}'' \times 9^{1}/_{4}''$ cardboard

- ❖ A needle or embroidery needle and thread

- ❖ Fabric (about $16'' \times 12''$)—an old dress, T-shirt, or pillowcase works well

- ❖ Eight pieces of $8^{1}/_{2}'' \times 11''$ plain white paper (for a longer book, you can use more paper)

- ❖ 1 piece of fancy or colored $8^{1}/_{2}'' \times 11''$ paper

- ❖ Wide packing tape and regular tape

- ❖ A ruler

- ❖ Fabric glue

- ❖ $12''$ ribbon

- ❖ Scissors

Fold the plain paper and the fancy paper in half. If the fancy paper looks different on the front than it does on the back, fold it so that the "front" side is on the inside. Put the folded plain paper inside the folded fancy paper, like a book. Then use your needle and thread to sew the papers together in two places, about an inch and a half from the top and an inch and a half from the bottom.

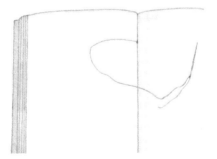

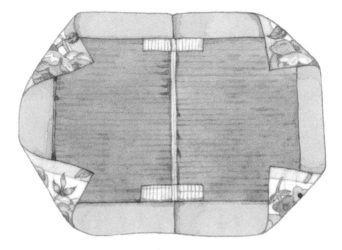

Cut your fabric to about 16 inches by 12 inches and lay it out, wrong-side facing up. Place the two pieces of cardboard in the middle of the fabric, leaving about a quarter of an inch between each piece. Tape the cardboard pieces together and maintain the quarter-inch separation. Coat the back of the cardboard lightly with fabric glue and then glue the cardboard to the cloth. Fold and glue each of the corners first and then fold and glue the fabric on each side. You can use tape to secure the fabric if necessary; just make sure the tape doesn't stick up close to the outer edge. Now you've made the fabric book cover.

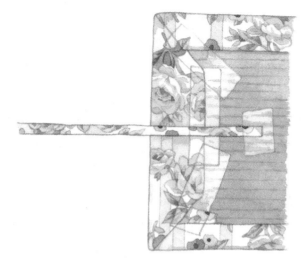

Cut your 12-inch ribbon in half. Use your ruler to find the center of the left side of your fabric cover and glue the end of one ribbon there (starting about two inches from the end of the ribbon). Try not to overglue, but also try to make sure you glue right to the very edge so that the ribbon is firmly attached. Secure with tape. Do the same thing on the right side of the cover with the other ribbon.

Open your papers and place them in the middle
of the cardboard and fabric so that the fold of the
paper is right in the center of the tape between
the cardboard pieces. Using the fabric glue, glue
the outer paper (the fancy paper) to the inside of
the cover and let it dry. Once dry, tie the ribbon
to close your book. It's not as secure as a lock
and key, but it's a pretty way to keep safe your
handmade journal, should you choose to use it
as a secret diary.

How to Skateboard

Go right ahead and jump on the skateboard and find your stance. It might be regular, with your left foot forward and your right foot at the back, ready to push. Or you might stand "goofy," which simply means you prefer to push with your left foot, so that's at the back. One stance will feel more comfortable than the other, and you can always change.

Skateboarding is all about change, confidence, and believing in what you've started. Relax. Keep your knees loose and bent. Trust what your body can do. Wear some pads (elbows and knees, and wrist guards). Use a helmet, no questions asked, one that covers that back of your head (a bike helmet doesn't really do the trick, but it's better than nothing). If skateboarding becomes your thing, skate shoes can be useful, because the bottoms are wider and flatter and have special strength in all the parts most likely to drag

on the ground and wear out. Above all, to skateboard is to experiment, to have fun, to try new things. It's not about rules; it's about you and your vision of moving along the ground and through the air.

To push off: Your front toes and foot are over the front truck, your back foot pushes off the ground—a few times, most likely. Once the skateboard starts to roll, pull the back foot up to rest over the back truck. Both feet turn to face the side as you glide. To push off again, pivot your feet to face forward. You will constantly shift from toes-facing-forward to toes-facing-sideways, and soon it will feel easy. You'll also learn to sway your hips, twist your shoulders, and bend your knees to keep the board moving.

Feet forward

Feet face side

That's on level ground. As soon as you start skateboarding downhill, you'll want some ways to stop. To foot break, face the front toes forward and put your weight on your front leg. Lower your back leg to the ground and drag it lightly along the ground, increasing the pressure until you stop. (Push too hard or too fast, and you'll fall.) To heel drag, move the back heel off the tail of the skateboard, lean back until the nose of the board pops into the air, and grind the back heel into the ground. Of course, you can always jump! Crouch, jump, and jog alongside as you land. If you jump forward, the board should stop in place.

To carve, or turn, lean your upper body in the direction you want to turn. Let your body feel it: push your heels down, bend your knees into a deep crouch, use your arms. Soon you'll be able to and work your way between slalom cones or any obstacle in your way. If you're headed downhill, carve from side to side, much like skiers carve their way down mountainsides to keep their momentum under control. Another way to turn is by resting your weight on the back leg and foot, lifting the front wheels lightly off the ground, and moving the nose of the skateboard left or right before lowering the front wheels to the ground. You can practice this move on a carpet or on grass, stepping on the tail while pushing the nose in a 360° circle.

The *Ollie* is a basic skateboarding trick—all four wheels of the skateboard lift off the ground, with no hands holding the board. It looks like magic, but here's how to do it: Start with your back foot on the tail and the front foot in the middle of the board. With your back foot, slam the board into the ground hard. Really believe in what you're doing and snap that board down. Then, do two movements pretty much at the same time: With your weight on your back foot, slide your front foot (which had been in the middle of the deck) toward the nose as—here comes the second movement—you jump your back leg

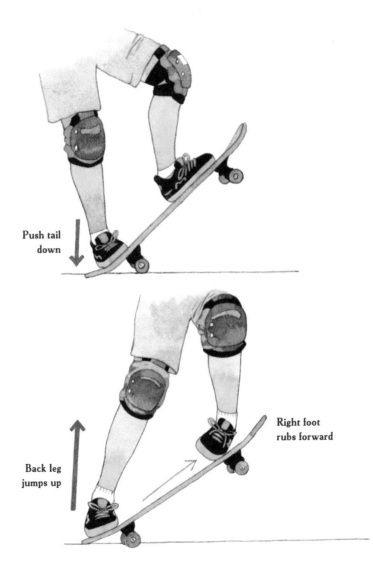

Push tail
down

Back leg
jumps up

Right foot
rubs forward

HOW TO SKATEBOARD

**Level out
in the air**

Land!

HOW TO SKATEBOARD

into the air, where it will join your already-raised front leg. You'll need to really jump—get those feet up, propel your body into the air, lift your knees to your chest. The skateboard's nose is up, your whole body will rise, the tail will lift, and for a brief and amazing moment you and the board will be suspended in midair. Get into a crouch position to absorb the impact of landing.

Yes, getting an Ollie takes practice. Daring girls know the two hundred times rule, that most things worth doing take patience, and there's little we can't do after practicing two hundred times. Skateboarding is like that too, although in the case of learning how to Ollie, it might take a thousand tries to feel the glory.

But you will, and then you'll be ready to jump sidewalk curbs, work a ramp, and, if you wish, enter the land of Wallie Five-O's, kickflips, manuals, and noseslides. You might even try a ripstick, which is a skateboard with two wheels, or just enjoy your newfound ability to travel farther and faster than before on your own four wheels.

෧

Playing Cards: Hearts and Gin

A SHORT HISTORY

Early playing cards are believed to have originated in China, where paper was first invented, as a form of paper dominoes. The earliest references to playing cards in Europe featuring decks with four suits date from 1377. Cards back then were very expensive, as they were hand-painted, and they looked quite different from the design of cards today.

The earliest cards from China had designs recognizable to players of Mah Jong: coins, or circles; and bamboo, or sticks. On their way from China to Europe, cards passed through the Islamic empire, where they gained cups, swords, and court cards. Once in Europe, the generic court cards evolved into depictions of actual kings, knights, and other royalty—hence the name "face cards." The Italian, Spanish, German, and Swiss cards did not include a queen—and in fact, even today, they still do not.

The basic familiar design of the cards—with hearts, diamonds, spades, and clubs, and court cards of Jacks, Queens, and Kings—came from France, and with the invention of woodcuts in the 14th century, mass-production became possible, making the French cards popular all across Europe. Cards became popular in America as well, and Americans began refining card design around 1800.

It was an American invention to create double-headed court cards, so that the kings, queens, and jacks never needed to be turned upright; to index the cards by placing the number and suit in the corner for easy reference; to varnish the surface of the cards for easier shuffling and durability; and to round the corners, which always seemed to get bent over anyway. It was in America, too, that the Joker was born, as a part of a card game called "Eucher," or sometimes "Juker." The Joker became an opportunity for satire—depicting popular political figures as jesters or clowns—and for advertising, which savvy marketers had already plastered on the back of the cards.

There are hundreds of games that can be played with cards. Here are two popular and fun games for four or two people: Hearts and Gin.

HEARTS

Hearts is a trick-taking game for four players in which the object of the game is to avoid winning tricks (a set of cards) containing Hearts or the Queen of Spades. Hearts began its life in Spain around 1750 in a game called Reverse, the point of which was to lose tricks, not gain them. Eventually, about 100 years later, Reverse fully morphed into the game we know today as Hearts.

"Tricks" are rounds of play in which each player puts a card face up on the table, and the player with the highest card wins all the cards—also called "trick-taking." But the real trick in this trick-taking game is that in Hearts, players want to avoid winning tricks, because the lowest score wins.

Hearts uses a standard 52-card deck. Aces are high, and there is no trump suit. To start, the dealer deals the cards clockwise so that all players have 13 cards each. Each player then chooses three cards to pass: on the first hand, the cards are passed to the left; on the next hand, the cards are passed right; on the third hand, cards are passed across; and on the fourth hand, no cards are passed. Cards are passed stacked face-down, and players must choose and pass their cards to the correct player before they can look at the cards passed to them.

The player who has the 2 of Clubs goes first and must "lead," or put down, that card. The play goes clockwise, with all the other players following suit (putting down a card of the same suit), if possible. That means each player must put down a Clubs card—if a player doesn't have any Clubs in this first hand, she can play any other card except for a Heart or the Queen of Spades. The player with the highest card takes the trick (stacking the cards face down next to her) and starts the next round. After the first trick, a Heart or the Queen of Spades can be used if a player doesn't have a card in the suit being led. Hearts can only be led (that is, be the first card in a trick) after a Heart has been "broken"—played on a trick where a player couldn't follow suit.

Play continues until all the cards have been played. Then you add up the points for each player. Each Heart card gets 1 penalty point, and the Queen of Spades gets 13 penalty points. The game is over when at least one person has 100 points or more, and the winner is the player with the lowest score.

But there is one last "trick" to be played in Hearts: a player can do something called "Shooting the Moon." That is when one player takes all the point cards (all Hearts and the Queen). The player who does this has her points reduced to zero, and everyone else automatically gets 26 points added to their score.

GIN RUMMY

This two-player card game is said to have been created by a man named Elwood T. Baker, who was inspired by an 18th-century game called Whiskey Poker. Gin rummy became popular in America in the 1930s, when Hollywood stars began playing the game in much the same way that celebrity poker is played today.

To play the game, you need a standard 52-card deck, and a pen and a pad of paper to keep score. You also need to know a bit of card talk to understand the game (see box on page ??).

To play

Decide who will be the dealer. The dealer then deals 10 cards to each of the two players and places the remaining cards in a stack between the players. Another card is placed face-up, next to the deck, to create a discard pile.

The goal of gin is to try to get your 10 cards grouped in melds—sequences of cards (three or more cards of the same suit in order) or sets of cards (three or four cards of the same value). Before you take a turn, check to see if you have any melds, or any groups of cards that could easily turn into melds.

GIN VOCABULARY

Combination
Two cards of the same rank, such as 2-2; or consecutive in the same suit, such as 2-3 of Clubs.

Count
The point value in a hand after deducting the total melded cards.

Deadwood
Cards that are not a part of any meld.

Gin
Ten melded cards.

Knock
To end the round.

Layoff
Getting rid of deadwood by incorporating it into the other player's melds, so that it is not counted.

Meld
Either a sequence or a set.

Sequences
A group of three or more cards of the same suit in consecutive order, such as 3-4-5 of Spades, or 8-9-10-J of Hearts.

Sets
A group of three or four cards of the same rank, such as 3-3-3 or J-J-J-J.

Each turn involves taking a card and discarding a card. The player who goes first draws a card from the deck. Now she must discard, choosing a card from her hand that is least likely to become part of a meld. High-point cards, like face cards, are good to discard if you can, since getting rid of them decreases your deadwood (the cards that are not part of any meld). Aces are low in this game: face cards are worth 10 points each, Aces are 1 point, and the other cards are equal to their numerical values (a 2 card of any suit is worth 2 points, a 3 card is 3 points, etc.).

When a player discards, the card must be placed face-up on the discard pile. The other player then has a turn, and she can draw from either the deck or the discard pile. Continue taking turns until a player "knocks," or until only 2 cards remain in the deck (in which case the hand ends in a draw).

Knocking is when a player ends the round, and is signaled by a player literally making a knocking sound on the table. A player can only knock if she has 10 points of deadwood or less. If you have 0 points of deadwood, also known as "going gin," you must knock. Otherwise, you don't have to knock unless you want to—even if you have 10 points in deadwood or less, you can keep playing to try for gin or for a lower point count.

When you decide to knock, rap once on the table, lay down your cards face up, and add up your deadwood. The other player then lays down her hand and separates her deadwood from her melds. If she has any deadwood that can be incorporated into your melds, she can "layoff"—that is, give them to you for your meld so they cannot be counted as her deadwood. After that, add up her total remaining deadwood. Subtract your deadwood from the other player's deadwood, and the answer you get is your score for this hand.

If you have 0 points of deadwood, you must knock and call "gin." You get a 25-point bonus for gin, on top of the points for the other player's deadwood (which she cannot layoff in this case).

If you knock and it turns out the other player has less deadwood than you, you get no points—but the other player scores not only the total of your deadwood minus hers, but 25 bonus points as well. That is called "under-cutting."

After the cards have been counted and points totaled, gather up the cards, shuffle, and deal the next hand.

Keep playing until one of the players reaches 100 points. Each player receives 25 points for each hand she won, and the player who reached 100 points first gets an extra 100-point bonus. The winner is the player with the most points after all the bonuses have been added.

⁂

How to Paddle a Canoe

There are larger, faster and more complex boats than a canoe, kayak, or raft, but in none of those fancier boats can you feel the water so closely, touch the mussels that cling tight in willow shoals, or slip into creeks and shallow wetlands to drift silently alongside cormorants, osprey, and swan.

Paddling a boat is an art that, like most pursuits, just needs practice to master. Huck Finn may have floated the Mississippi on a raft, and white-water kayaking is a thrill, but short of those, nothing beats a canoe for a water adventure.

Sometimes you need to be alone, and your canoe is there for you. Other times you want to adventure with a friend, and canoeing together is an exhilarating lesson in teamwork.

To learn to canoe, you should know these basic boat words, strokes, and concepts.

The ordinary canoe stroke is the *forward stroke*. To paddle on the right, grab the grip (or top knob of the paddle) with your left hand, and the shaft with your right. Put the paddle into the water, perpendicular to the boat, and pull it back and then out of the water. Keep your arms straight and twist your torso as you paddle. To paddle on the left, hold the grip with your right hand, the shaft with your left, and repeat.

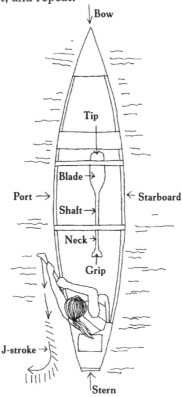

HOW TO PADDLE A CANOE

To change course and return from whence you came, turn the boat, and then paddle forward in the new direction. *The back stroke,* then, merely causes the boat to slow, or even stop. Put the paddle in the water slightly back, near the line of your hips, and pull toward the front, and then out.

It's important to remember that a canoe is not a bicycle. If you turn bicycle handlebars to the right, the bike will turn rightward. Not so in a canoe. When you paddle to the right, the boat will shift left. The opposite is true, too: left paddling pushes the boat to the right. Rotate your body as you paddle, since the power comes not from your arms, exactly, but from your torso. With practice, you will learn to do this instinctively, using your hips and body weight to control the boat's direction.

❧

Two-person canoeing is a delicate dance whereby the person at stern steers and gives directions while the person at bow paddles, changing sides at will to keep the boat in its line.

When you paddle alone it is essential to know the J-

stroke, which, by means of a small flip at the end, keeps the boat in a straight line. The J-stroke is just that. As you paddle on the left side, draw the letter J (see the canoe illustration). On the right side, it will look like a mirror-image J, or a fishhook. In other words, put the paddle in the water close to the canoe, and before your forward stroke ends, turn the paddle out and away from the boat; that's the J. Then lift the paddle out of the water, and ready it to start again.

Some beginning canoers constantly move the paddle from right to left sides, but that's a quick way to tire your arms. Using a *C-stroke* to steer will allow you to paddle to one side more of the time. Start as with a forward stroke, but trace a C (on the left, or its mirror image on the right) in the water. When you do this, turn the blade so it's nearly parallel to the water.

This next stroke has many names, crossback being one of them. It's a stop. Drag the blade into the water and hold it still. Really, really hold the paddle tight against the water's rush. This stops the boat. It also turns it to that side, but this is not a suggested way to turn, since it slows the boat down too much.

One final stroke is perfect for when you find yourself

in a cove with no company other than a family of sea otters and two seals nestling on the nearby rock. The quietest possible stroke will break no water and make no sound. Put the paddle in the water and keep it there, making a figure eight, over and again.

Now, in the big scheme of life, all you need is a boat

and a paddle. In real life, some additional gear is essential, the first being a lifejacket. It's itchy and annoying and you'll be tempted to leave it on shore. Don't. Please. It will save your life in a storm. In a less dire circumstance, if you tip, it will give you a leg up as you grab your paddle and pull yourself into your boat.

Drinking water is necessary, and, last but not least, bring a rope. Ropes are key to canoe adventures. You might find a stray canoe that needs to be towed to shore, or need to tie the canoe to a tree while you explore a riverbank. Perhaps the tide has gone out in a creek and you need to hop out of the boat and pull your canoe back to deeper waters. Lifejacket, water, rope, and you're set.

Last tips: In general, the closer to the boat you paddle, the straighter it will go. To turn, paddle farther from the boat. Crouch low in the boat when getting in and out. Read the tide charts so you know where the water is. Breathe deep, paddle smart, and enjoy your voyage.

❧

Marco Polo and Water Polo

Access to a pool, lake, pond, creek, river, stream, ocean, or garden hose is critical on a hot summer day. Contests are always fun: swimming stroke races (on your mark, get set, go!), diving, and seeing who can make up the funniest jumps. To do a cannonball, run off the diving board, hurl into the air, grab onto your legs, and make a huge splash. Underwater tricks like handstands and multiple back flips are also a nice way to cool off (and show off), as are attempts to mimic the intricacies of synchronized swimming. On a rainy day, you can watch old movies by water-ballet star Esther Williams for inspiration.

With water games, the main challenge is usually not the game itself, at least once you're on your way to mastering swimming—it's your nose, and how to keep water from rushing into it. You have three choices:

1. Breathe out sharply through your nose as you jump or duck underwater. The air coming out of your nose will keep water out.

2. Use one hand to hold your nose.

3. Find yourself an old-fashioned nose plug, the kind attached to the front of a rubber necklace. Clip your nose shut.

Thus prepared, following are a couple of aquatic games for those who can get to a pool or other slow-moving body of water.

MARCO POLO

The famed explorer Marco Polo was seventeen when he left Venice, Italy, to join his dad and uncle on a horseback journey to China. He did not return home for twenty-four years. While traveling, he befriended the Emperor Kublai Khan and was one of the first Western travelers of the Silk Road. He was fascinated by China's use of paper money and its intricate postal delivery system, innovations that far outstripped Europe's development at the time.

How Marco Polo's name got attached to the internationally known pool game, no one knows, but here are the rules.

You need at least three kids, and everyone starts in the water. One person is It, and her goal is to tag the other kids. She closes her eyes, thus blinded (or you can use your handy bandana for a blindfold). Then she counts to five, or whatever number you all agree on. To try to find the other kids without seeing them, It must listen and sense where they are. Whenever she wants, she yells "Marco." Everyone in the game must immediately respond "Polo." The girl who is It uses the sounds of the other kids' movements and voices to find and tag someone. Whomever she tags becomes the new It.

Variations

There are some alterations you can employ to make Marco Polo even more amusing and challenging. If you choose to, you can allow "fish out of water." This means the non-It kids can get out of the pool. However, at any time, It can yell "fish out of water" and if someone is out of the pool, that person automatically becomes the new It. If no one is out of the water, the other players often yell "no." (Hint: This can help It reorient and find them, too.)

You can also allow "mermaid on the rocks," which is similar to "fish out of water." If someone is a mermaid on the rocks, she is sitting on the ledge of the pool or the lakeshore with only her feet in the water. Again, if It yells "mermaid on the rocks," any mermaid becomes the new It. For either of these out-of-the-water variations, if It calls for fish or mermaids and there are none, she must do the start-of-game countdown again.

Another fun addition is "alligator eyes," which allows It to call out "alligator eyes" (or "submarine," if you prefer) and then swim underwater with eyes open for one breath. Usually It is allowed to use this only once. We've heard of some places where It is allowed to go underwater and look around any time, but cannot move until she is above water with eyes closed or blindfold on again. We haven't played this one, but you may want to try it.

Other Marco Polo variations are popular in different places throughout the globe. In Argentina, kids play a version where It has to say the name of whoever she tags. If she is right, the tagged person becomes It, but if she is wrong, she remains It and starts her countdown again. In California, they play "Sharks and Minnows" (called "Silent Witness" other places), which means there is no call and respond, just the sounds of kids moving in the water.

WATER POLO

While Marco Polo can thank the real Marco Polo for its name. water polo's comes from the game's rubber ball, which came from India via Tibet, where the word for ball is *pulu,* hence polo.

Water polo was invented in England in the 1870s, though a similar kind of game may have been played in rivers in Africa, and in flooded rice paddies in China, many centuries before. While water polo claimed to resemble rugby, in practice it was more akin to underwater wrestling, with players hitting and dunking each other underwater with great regularity. Players would protect the ball by sticking it in their swimsuit and swimming underwater toward the goal. A much-loved but extremely dangerous water polo feat had one player jumping off the backs of teammates, and flying through the air, ball in hand, toward the opposing goal.

Good thing the more civilized "Scottish" rules replaced the former free-for-all. The new rules instituted fouls for pushing and hitting, declared that the ball had to stay above water (no more bathing-suit tricks!), and stated that only a player holding the ball can be tackled (thus lowering the number of players who ended the game in the emergency room).

How to Play

A water polo team has six field swimmers and a goalie. Teammates pass the ball and keep it from the other side, until one of them can lob it into the goal and score. To move forward in water polo you swim with your head out of water, since you'll need to see where the ball is. To backstroke, you sit in the water, use your arms to make small short strokes, and use the eggbeater kick to stay up and moving: as you sit in the water, bend your knees, and circle each leg toward the other, like an eggbeater.

Rules

◆ You can touch the ball with your hands— though with only one hand at a time, which means you'll catch the ball and pass it quickly.

- ♦ Don't touch the bottom of the pool. This sport is about constant motion, no rest, and never touching bottom.

- ♦ No pushing, pulling, hitting, or holding on to the other players—that's a foul. Fouls also are called if you hold the ball under water, touch it with two hands, or hold onto it longer than 35 seconds; or if you touch bottom, push off the side of the pool, or use bad language.

While Marco Polo will never be an Olympic sport, water polo is. Male Olympians have played water polo since 1900. Ever since the 2000 Summer Olympics in Sydney, women's water polo has been on the roster, too, and there's a terrific story behind its entry. After a decade or two of polite behind-the-scenes negotiation with the International Olympic Committee, the Australian women's national water polo team pushed the issue. The upcoming Olympics were on their turf, after all, and they wanted to compete. In 1998, members of the Olympic leadership were set to arrive at the Sydney airport, in town for a planning visit. Led by their goalkeeper Liz Weekes—she's called the team's "glamour girl" because she's also a model—the Aussie women water polo players put on their swimsuits and caps and strode through the Sydney airport to meet them, and, very much in the public eye, they asked again to be included, and met with success.

Better yet, after fighting so hard to be included, the Australian women's team won the gold medal, with player Yvette Higgins scoring the winning goal during the last second of the championship game, to the applause of fans who filled the stadium.

࿐

Drawing a Face

Drawing is something you can do whether you're outside under a shady tree or inside listening to a summer rainstorm. All you need is paper, a pencil and eraser, and your imagination.

1. Make an oval.

2. Draw a line down the center of the oval from top to bottom. This guideline and the other lines you will be drawing in the next four steps should be dark enough to see but faint enough to be easily erased.

3. A little more than halfway down, draw a straight line across. (This will be where the eyes will go.)

4. Halfway between that line and the bottom of the oval, draw another line. (This will be where the nose ends.)

5. Draw another line halfway between the line you just drew and the bottom of the oval. (This will be where the mouth goes.)

6. Starting at the bottom of the oval and extending downward, draw two lines for the neck.

7. Using the lines you've made as guides, start sketching in the eyes, nose, and mouth. Once you're happy with what you have, sketch in the hair.

8. To make sure your drawing is symmetrical, hold it up to a mirror. Crooked or lopsided areas tend to jump out at you when you look at your work "backwards."

9. When you've corrected any lopsidedness, and you're happy with the general look of the face you've drawn, you can start to erase those guiding lines you made at the beginning and either continue to refine your work or bask in a job well done.

TIPS FOR DRAWING ANYTHING

Use Relative Proportions

Use your thumb or your pencil as a measuring stick to gauge the length and distance of what you're drawing. If you're drawing the tree in your backyard, for instance, close one eye and hold up a thumb. When you hold your thumb next to the tree, is the trunk as long as your thumb? Twice as long? Is the treetop the same, or less, or more? Once you compare those measurements, you can apply them to your drawing to help create more accurate proportions.

Use a Grid

If you're working from a picture, instead of trying to attack the whole scene all at once, divide it into a grid of one-inch squares. You can do this by drawing a grid on a sheet of clear plastic (or, in a pinch, on clear plastic wrap) to lay over your reference material, or by cutting up a piece of paper into one-inch squares, laying them out over your picture or photo, and removing one square at a time to reveal that one-inch square portion of the photo below. Divide the workspace of your sketchpad into a grid as well and transcribe what you see, one square at a time.

Draw Upside Down

Just like holding your artwork up to a mirror, drawing something upside down makes everything familiar look new and even a little strange. But that's a good thing, because it tricks your brain into breaking things down into basic shapes and patterns instead of automatically recognizing and categorizing what you see. When you think, "I'm going to draw a nose," your brain is filled with everything it already knows about what noses look like—including what a "bad drawing" of a nose looks like. And that may inhibit you from drawing to the best of your ability. When you look at a picture of a nose upside down and try to draw it, you're forced to rely on what you see—which certainly doesn't look like what your brain knows about noses. So you have to instead follow your instinct in replicating what you see. A rounded part here, a dark part here, a straight line there. Not a lot of opportunity for a chattery brain to jump in with a critique. Try this with a line drawing first: Take a page from an old coloring book, place it upside down in front of you, and try to draw what you see. (For a fun experiment, try drawing the same picture from the page right side up. Which one looks more like the original picture?)

Knots and Stitches

A good knot assures that your boat will be there when you return, your tire swing will hold, and your dog won't run into traffic. Here are a few knots with many everyday uses, and a few words on stitches, which come in handy for small repairs.

A piece of rope is all you need to begin. In each of our directions, "rope" means the stable or standing part of the rope. "End" refers to the part you are working with to make the knot, the working end. Make sure it's always long enough to do the job. "Bight" is another word worth knowing; it's the part of the rope that becomes the knot.

1. STOPPERS

A stopper knot keeps a rope from slipping through a hole; it is the bulge at the end of a line. The most ordinary kind is called the overhand knot, or half knot. It's the knot you use to keep a thread in place when you start to sew.

Half knots are not very strong, but they are perfect for making the swing part of a rope swing. Tie four or five loose half knots near the bottom of the rope. Push them together, and tighten. They'll form a larger bulb that's perfect for sitting on as you swing. If you like, tie a half knot every few feet up the rope, for climbing or for holding on to while you do an arabesque (twisting the rope slightly around one ankle, and lifting your other leg gracefully behind you, like they do at the circus).

Safety note: For rope swings, you'll want to attach the swing to a tree branch using a stronger clove hitch or a tautline hitch. Make sure you tie the rope to a branch that extends far enough from the trunk so you can swing safely.

An alternative to the half knot is the **Flemish knot,** which you can also use any time you need a knot at the end of a line. It's both strong and lovely.

① Make a loop at the top. **②** Cross the end in back and over to the left. **③** Wrap the end over and into the eye of the initial loop. You should see a figure eight. **④** Pull the end into the eye, or center, of that loop. **⑤** Pull tight.

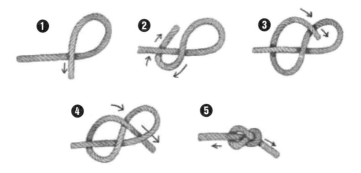

2. LOOPS

Once you've mastered the Flemish figure eight, you can make a loop the same way. Double up the rope or string. For hauling, tie the loop around your object, and lift or drag with the rope.

3. BENDS

Bends link two ropes together. When you need to repair a string that's broken, add new length to a rope, or for any reason tie two ropes together, the square knot is what you want. Also called the Hercules knot, it was used by the Greeks and Romans as a healing charm. In *Natural History,* the Roman writer Pliny the Elder advised people to tie off their bandages with this knot, since it would heal the wound more quickly. Simple and reliable, this knot works best on twine or thinner rope, and with any ropes of equal size.

The classic formulation for a **square knot** is this: Left over right, right over left. Don't worry: In our experience, that's the kind of direction that makes more sense after you already know how to tie knots. So, try this: Loop **Ⓐ** over loop **Ⓑ**. Wrap the ropes of **Ⓑ** over the sides of, and into, loop **Ⓐ**. Pull.

Square Knot

If you're attaching the ends of a single rope, perhaps to tie off a friendship bracelet, try this: Make loop **Ⓐ**. With loop **Ⓑ**, thread the end into loop **Ⓐ**, from the back. Then weave it out the bottom side, and under and across to the top of the loop. Next, bring rope **Ⓐ** over the top side and through the loop, so it's next to the other side of rope **Ⓑ**.

If you need something stronger, or your ropes are different sizes, use this variation, the **sheetbend knot.** The green one is the thicker rope.

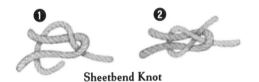

Sheetbend Knot

4. HITCHES

Hitches tie an object or animal to a post, whether it's your dog at a friend's house, your horse to a tree in the shade, or your kayak to a pole on the dock while you go for a swim.

The **tautline hitch** is incredibly useful on camping and boating trips. Here's how to make it:

❶ Start from the back and bring the end around the pole to the front, ❷ then over and behind the rope and ❸ into the center, or eye, and out the front. ❹ Pull the end over and behind and into the center once again, and ❺ pull out the front and ❻ tighten. ❼ Take the end past the first two loops, and ❽ wind it over and behind and into the center. ❾ Pull through and ❿ up to tighten.

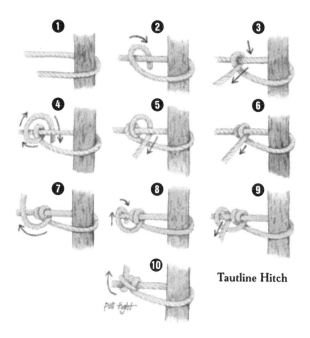

Tautline Hitch

The **around-the-pole hitch** moves around a pole. This is perfect for a dog who doesn't want to end up tangled, twisted, and stuck with a two-inch leash.

Loop the end one turn around the pole, front to back, and bring the end under and in front of the rope. Change course and lead it toward the top.

Wrap the end again around the pole, this time back to front, and then lead the end under and through the loop.

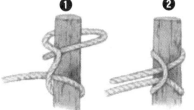

Around-the-Pole Hitch

Finally, the **timber hitch** helps you drag a heavy object, like a log across a field. This knot is simple and also easy to untie, an important consideration in knots. It tightens in the direction you pull in, so make sure to use that to your advantage.

Wrap one turn, top to bottom, back to front. At the top, loop the end around the rope, to the left (this loop is important; the end must be wrapped around the rope it just came from). Tuck the end over, back, and around three or four times, and pull tight. The tucks must sit flat against the object for this knot to stay tight, since it is held in place by the rope's pressure against the object as you pull.

Timber Hitch

5. STITCHES

There will no doubt come a time when you need to mend your gloves, replace a button that's fallen off, or sew the tear your pants suffered while climbing rocks.

Cut your thread, push it through the needle, double the thread so it's extra strong, and place a knot—a gorgeous Flemish stopper knot—at the end. You're ready. The stitches below can help you quickly mend any rip or tear that will inevitably occur in a daring life.

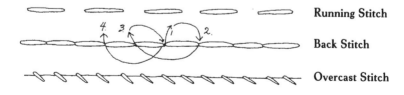

Running Stitch

Back Stitch

Overcast Stitch

Lemonade Stand

A lemonade stand is a great way to earn a little spending money and meet your neighbors. What you need:

- ❦ Lemonade, in a pitcher or large thermos
- ❦ Ice (and a cooler to keep it frozen)
- ❦ Snacks
- ❦ Cups and napkins
- ❦ Change box, or the cash register you played with in kindergarten, if your little sister hasn't broken it
- ❦ Folding card table
- ❦ Big sign, most definitely, and a price list
- ❦ Chairs or a bench, if you'd like
- ❦ Optional: Music, or another way to call attention to the stand

Lemonade and brownies are a classic combination. Baking brownies from a box is quick work, and we've included recipes for other treats as well.

Crafts are good, too—perhaps friendship bracelets, which you can work on between customers. You might also devote half the table to a mini yard sale, and sell odds-and-ends you've outgrown. This is where the card table's size comes in handy.

RECIPES FOR YOUR STAND

Lemonade

If you want to squeeze fresh lemons, here's the basic recipe, which yields 4 cups. You can see that making enough fresh lemonade for your stand will entail much lemon-juicing time.

- ❦ 4 cups of water
- ❦ Juice from 6 lemons
- ❦ ¾ cup of sugar, or more, depending on whether you prefer sweet or tart lemonade

Mix together by hand or in a blender, adjust sweetness, and serve over ice.

Alternately, you can make lemonade from frozen lemonade concentrate, available at the grocery, or from dry mix. There's nothing wrong with these not-from-scratch options, especially if the idea is to get out to the street and sell some lemonade, not stand at the kitchen counter all morning juicing lemons. Follow the directions on the can or bag. You can always cut some thin lemon slices, and add one to each cup of lemonade you pour.

Lemon Candy Straw Treats

To make this old-fashioned treat, push a lemon candy stick (these are hollow inside) into the open side of a lemon that's been cut in half. The combo of the tart lemon and the sweet stick is perfect.

To make this treat from a whole lemon, use an apple corer, lemon juicer, or a sharp knife to make a hole for the candy straw. You can also use oranges or limes.

Baked Goods

Shortbread makes an excellent and unexpected addition to any full-service lemonade stand, as does fudge. Both recipes are incredibly easy, although fudge will take fore-thought, as it needs two hours or so in the refrigerator to become firm.

Shortbread

- ❦ 1 cup of sugar
- ❦ 1 cup of butter (equals two sticks, or ½ pound)
- ❦ 3 cups of all-purpose flour

Preheat the oven to 275 degrees. Cream the sugar and butter. Measure in 2½ cups of flour, and mix thoroughly. Flour a tabletop, counter, or wooden board with the left-over ½ cup of flour, and knead until you see cracks on the dough's surface. Roll out the dough to ¼ inch thick, and cut into squares, bars, or any shape you wish. With a fork, prick the cookies, and put them on an ungreased cookie sheet. Bake for 45 minutes, until the tops are light brown. You can also add almonds, hazelnuts, or choco-late chips to the dough if you like.

Fudge

- ❦ 2 packages, or 16 squares, of semi-sweet baking chocolate
- ❦ 1 can of sweetened condensed milk, the 14-ounce size
- ❦ 1 teaspoon vanilla

Melt the chocolate with the condensed milk, either in a microwave for 2–3 minutes, or on top of the stove. The chocolate should be almost but not entirely melted. Stir, and the chocolate will melt fully. Add vanilla. Line a square pan (8 inches is a good size) with wax paper, and pour in the chocolate-milk-vanilla mixture. Chill for two hours or more if needed, until firm. Cut into bars or squares.

CALCULATING YOUR PROFIT

If you are working your lemonade stand to save up dollars for a Swiss Army knife or a special book, you must understand how to figure out how much you earned—that is, your profit. Let's say you make the expanded-version lemonade stand. From the sale of lemonade, fudge, and three Beanie Babies, you earned $32.

First figure the profit, using this standard equation:

Revenue (money taken in) –
Expenses (food, drink, etc.) = **Profit**

Revenue: You sold 30 cups of lemonade and 20 pieces of fudge, charged 50 cents for each item and earned $25. Plus, someone paid you $7 for those Beanie Babies your great aunt brought for your second birthday. At the end of the day you took in $32.

Expenses:

3 cans of frozen lemonade	2.50
38 plastic cups	1.50
fudge ingredients	2.00
Total Expenses	6.00

Now plug the numbers into the equation: 32 minus 6 equals 26. You cleared $26 in profit.

Fry an Egg on the Sidewalk

If you've lived any amount of time in a very warm place, no doubt you've heard the weatherperson describe the summer temperatures as "so hot you could fry an egg on the sidewalk." That sounds very hot indeed. But is it really possible for the ground to be so hot a person could use it to cook breakfast?

We will be frank with you: the answer, sadly, is no. Unless you live in on the lip of a bubbling volcano, chances are that even though it feels so hot you could fry an egg, it's actually not quite hot enough.

FRY AN EGG ON THE SIDEWALK

A raw egg is a liquid, and when we cook it, it becomes a solid. But the egg has to reach anywhere from 144° to 158° Fahrenheit before that can happen. (Egg whites start to coagulate at 144° F; yolks coagulate at 149° F.) Even if you were on a sidewalk in Death Valley, where it's been as hot as 134° F, or in Libya, where the highest temperature on Earth, 136° F, was recorded in 1922, the ground still wouldn't be as hot as a frying pan. (Consider, too, that when you crack open a room-temperature cool egg onto a sidewalk that's 130° to 140° F, the egg itself cools the surface down.)

But there are a few tricks and tips that can make sidewalk egg-frying interesting, if not exactly edible. So, just on the off-chance that you are reading this on the hottest day of the year in the hottest place on earth, we present for you some tips on how to fry an egg on the sidewalk.

You Will Need:

- ✿ A hot day (100° F or warmer)
- ✿ A piece of tinfoil, about the same size as a small frying pan
- ✿ One egg
- ✿ A hot sidewalk or blacktop

WHAT TO DO

1. Make sure you are in an area where the sun is shining directly on you, and that the side-walk or blacktop is pedestrian-free.

2. Lay down your tin foil, shiny side up, and fold up the edges a few inches all the way around, both to keep the egg from running out and help redirect some of that sunlight.

3. Crack the egg onto the foil.

4. Wait.

HOW IT WORKS (OR DOESN'T)

Since the pavement itself isn't quite as hot as a stovetop, and since the coolness of the egg itself lowers the temperature of the sidewalk it's on, it is impossible to generate enough heat to really fry an egg to breakfast standards without a little extra help.

However, using a playground blacktop or the dark asphalt surface of a parking lot can heat things up a bit. (Dark colors absorb more light and more heat than lighter colors, and thus a blacktop or parking lot soaks up more of the sun's energy—and retains it longer—than a regular sidewalk.)

Also, using tinfoil, which not only conducts heat but reflects it, helps to capture and redirect the heat coming from the sun back into the egg itself. A well-placed magnifying glass or mirror can also harness the sun's solar energy to cook the egg.

BONUS TIP

If you are doing this experiment in your driveway and your parents' car is nearby, soaking up the sun, you might have another super-hot surface on hand that's much better suited to egg-frying. The hood, being metal, is a much better conductor of heat. So, if mom or dad says it's okay, get another egg, another good-sized piece of tinfoil, and try the experiment again, this time on the hood of the car.

BONUS WARNING

There is a fine line between daring and reckless, and we would be remiss if we did not remind you that you should NOT eat the results of your egg-on-sidewalk experiment. But if you have found your appetite whetted by this particular foray into science, you can always head on back inside and make some eggs the old-fashioned way—cooked, fully through, in a frying pan.

DID YOU KNOW?

Every year on the Fourth of July, the city of Oatman, Arizona, holds a Solar Egg Frying Contest where contestants have fifteen minutes to try to fry an egg using sun power.

Three Silly Pranks

Think boys are the only ones good at pranking? Think again! Here are three classic pranks for any daring girl.

STINK BOMBS

The old-fashioned kind, from the herb valerian.

Head outdoors with the following:

- a small jar with a screw-on lid
- measuring spoons
- any kind of vinegar you can snag from the kitchen
- valerian root powder—this is the key ingredient for a stink bomb. You can find this at any grocery store that stocks vitamins and herbal remedies. It comes in capsules that can be opened and emptied. If you can only find valerian tea, mash it into a powder.

Mix one or more teaspoons of the powder with 2 teaspoons of vinegar, close the jar very, very quickly and shake. When you're ready to set off the stink bomb, open the jar (don't throw it), yell "Skunk!" and run.

SHORT-SHEETING BEDS

For this prank you'll need to know the old-fashioned skill of making a bed, the fancy way, with tucked-in sheets.

Here's a refresher: Fit the bottom sheet over the mattress. Tuck the top sheet under the foot of the bed and along at least part of the sides. Lay the blanket on top, tuck that in too, and then neatly fold the top edge of the sheet over the blanket, about six inches or so. There. Stand back and observe your handiwork, because you will want the short-sheeted bed to look the same way.

To short-sheet a bed, you merely reposition the top sheet. Instead of tucking it in at the foot of the bed, tuck it in at the head of the bed. Lay out the sheet and halfway down the bed, stop and fold the sheet back toward the pillows. Place the blanket on top and fold a few inches of sheet on top for that neat, just-made look. This bed looks normal, but just try and stretch your legs out!

Important: Don't do this to anyone whose feelings will be hurt, only to those you know will laugh hard or at least giggle when they figure it out.

FAUX BLOOD

Fool your friends with this easily prepared hoax.

Needed:

- corn syrup
- cornstarch
- red food coloring from the pantry
- a jar with a tight lid
- a spoon
- an eyedropper

Red food coloring can stain, so wear old clothes, although washing with very warm water and strong soap should clean it up. It is best to keep this prank outdoors.

Mix 4 small drops of food coloring, 2 teaspoons of water, and 1 to 2 teaspoons of cornstarch in the jar, cover, and shake. Pour in 2 tablespoons of corn syrup. Cover and shake again.

Use an eyedropper or a spoon to drip the fake blood where you want it. Make up a good story.

∂o

Shooting a Basketball

Get your arms out in front, elbows bent. Your stronger arm holds the ball, the weaker supports it. Your hands are close together, with the fingers spread. Flick your wrist back, and push the ball into the air toward the net. Really push. For more fun, try a jump shot. Position yourself in classic ready position: two feet on the floor, legs slightly bent and shoulder-width apart, one foot slightly forward, and shoulders squared to the basket. Hold the ball with your arms and hands high and cock your wrists back. Aim for the backboard. When you shoot, stay relaxed, look at the rim, uncock your wrists—and push the ball into the air while you jump up and slightly back. The power from your legs pushes through to your arms and sends the ball high into the air toward the net. You will be able to score many more points over the outstretched hands of defenders if you can perfect this fade-away jump shot.

How to Look at a Leaf

Each tree has a unique and special leaf. Identifying an unfamiliar tree by its leaf means peering closely at its leaf, making note of distinctive features, consulting a good tree identification guide, and narrowing down the options to find a match. With over half a million species of trees in the world, and seven hundred in North America alone, you'll need to find a guidebook that is specific to your region. The following questions will speed you on the way to noticing details, like the difference between needles that always attach to a secondary stem, as in our illustration of an Eastern Hemlock, and needles that attach to secondary stems and to the primary stem too, like those of a Dawn Redwood. Spread some leaves out before you and start navigating your way around the incredible world of trees.

Dawn Redwood

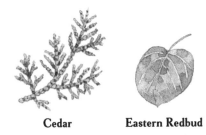

Cedar   **Eastern Redbud**

1. Is the leaf a needle like the Dawn Redwood?
   Made of overlapping scales like a Cedar?
   Or broad and flat like an Eastern Redbud?

2. If the leaf is a needle, are the needles single,
   like Hemlock, or clustered together, like the
   Corsican Pine? Do the needles lay flat, are
   they feathery, or are they four-sided, so that
   the branch rolls between your fingers? Are
   the ends pointy or wide? Are there white
   lines underneath, a sure sign of an Eastern
   Hemlock?

Eastern Hemlock   **Corsican Pine**

3. If the leaf is scaly like a Cedar, is the scale rounded, or flat?

4. If the leaf is broad and flat, is the arrangement simple, with one leaf attached to a stem, like the White Oak, or is it compound, with several leaflets to a stem? On the compound leaf, are the leaves placed opposite each other, like a White Ash, or are they alternate and asymmetrical?

White Oak

White Ash

5. The leaf's outline, or edge, is called the margin. Is it smooth and continuous, or toothy? Are the teeth small and close together, like the American Elm, or coarse, like a White Oak?

American Elm

Does each vein of the leaf end in a tooth?
Are the teeth all the same size?

6. Does the leaf have lobes, like the Sugar Maple's three lobes, and if so, how many, and how far apart? Are the spaces between the lobes—called lobe notches—V-shaped or U-shaped, deep or shallow? Are there extra notches on each lobe?

Sugar Maple

7. Is the top of the leaf pointy, triangular, wavy, or round? Is the base, where the leaf connects to the stem, squared off and flat, round, heart-shaped like the Quaking Aspen, or V-wedged like the White Oak? Are the sides of the top and base symmetrical, or do they vary? Is the stem long or short?

Quaking Aspen

8. Do the leaf's veins radiate directly from the stem, like fingers, or are they connected to a main vein that runs through the leaf?

Boxelder

Soon you will be noticing even smaller details than we've thought of here.

As you collect leaves and match them to trees, you might want to create a leaf fieldbook. It might be a book of your neighborhood's trees, or vacation-spot trees, or merely a way to save leaves to identify later. Leaves can be pressed and preserved in several ways. You can stick them between two pages of a book and weigh the book down for several days. You can follow the directions for making a wooden flower press (in *The Daring Book for Girls*), but use larger pieces of wood for the top and bottom (say, 12 by 12 inches).

Leaves can also be preserved in wax paper. Set the leaf between two pieces of wax paper and cover the pile with a thin towel. Turn the iron to medium hot, no steam, and iron over the towel to seal the wax paper around the leaf (ask an adult for help if you're not used to using a hot iron). The pages of wax-pressed leaves can be cut to a similar size, and bound together for your book.

With leaves, there's always the chance to revisit your own early childhood: remember crayon rubbings of the undersides of leaves? Try updating that with new materials, like better paper, compressed charcoal, and good-quality artist's pencils. There's also that elementary school science experiment, whereby the stem of a fallen leaf is placed into one half a cup of water mixed with ten drops of red food coloring (give the stem a fresh cut just before it hits the water), and everyone watches for three or four days until the veins and eventually the entire leaf turn red.

Making a Seine Net

A seine net is just a long fishing net used for dipping into the ocean to collect and study marine life.

What you need:

◆ Seine netting, often sold as minnow seine. Ours is 4 feet deep and 15 feet long, with a $1/8$ inch mesh, but these measurements are flexible, depending on how big or small you want your net to be, and what's available. It's nice when the net has a bit of Styrofoam at the top edge to keep it afloat, and some metal weights on the bottom to help it sink. Some seine netting comes this way. It can be bought at marine shops.

◆ Two 4-foot poles or lengths of wood, to control the net, and to wind it up when you're done.

◆ A large bucket, to keep your catch in water and to store the net.

Attach the shorter sides of the net to the poles. Do this by drilling a hole at each end of the pole (they might do this for you at a marine shop, if you ask). Or, use a Swiss Army knife to whittle a channel at each end of the pole, and wrap the rope there. Or forget the whittling and just wrap the rope very tight. If there's not already a thin rope at each corner of your net, find a small length of light rope or twine and use that.

One person stands at the shoreline and holds a pole. The other person holds the second pole and wades into the water until the net is fully extended. Keep the top at water level and let the rest of the net sink. This is where the metal weights come in handy.

After a time, walk back to shore in a sweeping motion, keeping the net fully extended so that when you get to shore, you'll be a net-length away from your friend or parent holding the other end of the net. As you get closer to shore, slowly change the net direction from vertical—where it is catching fish and other creatures—to horizontal, where you can scoop them up and lay out the net on the wet sand to see what you've got.

If you're not catching much of anything, change your position, or your location, or trawl some, walking around with the net stretched, giving more fish more time to end up in your hands. Both of you can walk farther into the river or surf.

Toss back everything within a few minutes so that your spider crabs, starfish, striped bass, tiny snails, and shiny minnows can continue their lives at sea. Many towns have laws that tell you to toss the sea animals back where they belong, or else you will suffer a stiff penalty.

(Some beaches ban large-scale commercial seine netting, but these small ones are usually okay.)

If you're going fishing, though, those little minnows are good bait.

HOW TO CLEAN A SHELL

When your beachcombing and seine netting land you choice shells, here are two ways to clean them and turn them into long lasting treasures.

1. Bury the shells 12 inches underground in your backyard and let the earthworms and all those soil bacteria do their work. This can take several months.

2. Boil for five minutes in a large pot, in a solution that is half water and half bleach. You'll see when the shells are clean. Take them out carefully with tongs, or ask someone older to do it, because the water is scalding. Rinse with cool water.

Tinikling (Bamboo Dance)

Tinikling (teeh-NEEHK-lihng), which means "bamboo dance," originated in the Leyte province of the Visayas Islands in the Philippines. The dance is meant to imitate the movements of the long-legged tikling (TEEK-lihng) bird as it moves through rice fields and swampy marshlands, trying to evade bamboo traps set by farmers. Dancers evoke the bird's movements by jumping and hopping between two horizontal bamboo poles, held and moved by other dancers. The original Tinikling folk dance is rather lengthy and complicated, but its basic steps can be mastered by anyone.

TINIKLING (BAMBOO DANCE)

You will need:

- ❧ At least three people (two to hold the bamboo poles, plus at least one dancer)
- ❧ Two 8- to 9-foot long poles made of bamboo (in a pinch, you can also use collapsible tent poles; whatever you substitute for bamboo, make sure it is flexible)
- ❧ Two blocks of wood (about 2 inches thick and 30 inches long)
- ❧ Optional: music with four-count beat. If you don't use music, it's helpful to chant the counts out loud to keep time.

For the dancers:

- ❧ Traditionally, the dance is performed with your hands on your hips, but you can also dance with your hands at your sides or behind your back.
- ❧ Always begin the dance on the left side (with your right shoulder nearest the poles).
- ❧ If you have two dancers, they can dance together— facing each other and holding hands, facing away from each other, even starting on opposite sides of the poles. Just make sure that the dancers keep

their arms close to their bodies so as not to knock each other over.

❧ Either do the dance barefoot (as it is traditionally performed), or make sure that the shoes you are wearing are securely fastened, with all laces tied.

❧ Practice the dance first without the poles moving to make sure you've got the steps down.

For those holding the bamboo poles:

❧ Sit on the ground across from each other, cross-legged, holding the ends of the poles.

❧ Place the two blocks of wood under the poles about a foot away from each end. (This will allow you to tap the poles down without banging your hands on the ground.)

❧ Make sure the poles are about as far apart from each other as your knees are when sitting cross-legged.

❧ When clapping the poles together, slide the poles toward each other to clap rather than lift them up. Otherwise the dancers may trip.

POLE PATTERN

Count 1: Clap poles together

Count 2: Clap poles together

Count 3: Tap poles down on the board

Count 4: Tap poles down on the board

DOING THE DANCE

Begin by standing to the left of the poles. The pole clappers can warm up by tapping out the four-count pattern (together, together, down, down). To prepare for the dance, the dancer can warm up by stamping her right foot outside the poles for the first two counts, then tapping her right foot between the poles for the second two counts. She can repeat this a few times before beginning the dance. There are many different kinds of steps in Tinikling; below are three basic steps that can be combined in any fashion and repeated as many times as you like.

SINGLE STEP
(two counts of 4)

Count 1: Hop on your left foot outside the poles, on the left side

Count 2: Hop again on your left foot

Count 3: Hop in between the poles with your right foot

Count 4: Hop between the poles again, this time using your left foot

Count 1: Hop to the outside right of the poles with your right foot

Count 2: Hop again on your right foot outside the poles

Count 3: Hop in between the poles with your left foot

Count 4: Hop between the poles again, this time using your right foot

Repeat from the top.

CROSSOVER STEP (two counts of 4)

Count 1: Hop on your left foot outside the poles (on the left side)

Count 2: Hop on your right foot outside the poles

Count 3: Cross your left foot over your right to step between the poles

Count 4: Step your right foot to the right side of the poles

Count 1: Hop on your right foot outside the poles (on the right)

Count 2: Hop on your left foot outside the poles

Count 3: Cross your right foot over your left to step between the poles

Count 4: Step your left foot to the left side of the poles

Repeat from the top.

DOUBLE STEP (two counts of 4)

Count 1: Hop on both feet (outside the poles on the left)

Count 2: Hop on both feet again

Count 3: Hop in between the poles with both feet

Count 4: Hop both feet again between the poles

Count 1: Hop both feet outside of the poles to straddle them (one foot on either side of the poles)

Count 2: Hop both feet outside poles again

Count 3: Hop both feet back in between the poles

Count 4: Hop both feet again between the poles

Repeat from the top, this time starting from the right

Clubhouses and Forts

Every girl should have a clubhouse or fort of her own, and here are some ideas for making one. Several weekends may be spent sweating over the plans for a long-lasting clubhouse of wood beams and nails and real roofing tile. But there are ways to make quicker work of this endeavor.

QUICK FORT

With 6-foot metal garden stakes, you can construct an outdoor clubhouse or fort almost immediately. Garden stakes haven't the stability of wood beams, but the swiftness with which the walls go up easily makes up for that. Five stakes will do the trick.

The stakes come with footholds. Stand on them and they should push into the ground rather effortlessly. If there's a problem, a rubber mallet or a taller person can help; if the problem proves intractable, that may mean that there's a rock in the ground and you need to move the stake. Use one stake for each of the four corners. Set the fifth stake along one of the sides to create a space for the door.

Wrap the whole structure, except the doorway, with chicken wire or deer netting, or lighter-weight bird netting. Garden stakes have notches in them and you can attach the materials to the notches to form the basic wall. (Trim the bottom of the netting neatly at ground level, lest chipmunks and other small animals inadvertently get tangled inside; this happened to us.)

To add privacy, use burlap or a white painter's dropcloth as a second layer, or cardboard (you'll figure a way to attach these to the stakes). If you want a ceiling, the burlap or dropcloth will help, although they won't be waterproof, and rainwater will collect on top. You can use a tarp, but the plastic can make the inside very hot. You'll figure it out. A sixth stake, taller than the rest, can be added to the center to create a sloped ceiling. From here, use twine, rope, duct tape, wire, scissors, sticks, cardboard, plywood, and any other wood scraps you can scare up to build walls, create windows, ceilings and floors, and otherwise make it your own. There are no rules; it's your fort.

LEAN-TO

A lean-to is a very primitive form of shelter that's little more than a wall or two and a roof. It's meant to keep you safe from the worst of the rain and wind, and often leans into existing walls or fences, hence the name. Find any tucked-in spot or corner, rig a tarp roof with some ropes knotted to trees, and lean a side of plywood against the house. Build up the front with branches, odd pieces of old fence your neighbors left out on trash day, or even a picnic table turned on its side.

INDOOR FORT

The classic formula of couch cushions, blankets, pillows, and the backs of sofas and chairs is a good start for an indoor fort, as is throwing a large blanket over the top of the dining room table (stacks of books on top help keep them in position) and letting the long sides drape down.

You can improve upon these traditional forts. To make a hanging wall, screw a line of hooks or eyebolts into the ceiling. Run picture-hanging wire or clothesline rope through them. Attach clips or clothespins, and from these, dangle all sorts of sheets, light blankets, large swaths of cloth, holiday lights, or your mother's oversized scarves to create a different kind of fort.

How to Make a Pillowcase Skirt

Whether you're stuck inside on a rainy day and itching for a craft, or simply looking for a new style to wear while you play tag outside, this is a quick way to whip up a new look. Since one end of the pillowcase is already finished and sewn nicely, all you have to do is cut the other end and put in a drawstring. And for true girl-on-the-go clever crafting, you can use washable fabric glue and forget the needle and thread altogether. Here's one way to do it.

You will need:

- ❦ A pillowcase
- ❦ Scissors
- ❦ An iron
- ❦ One ribbon, long enough to circle your waist twice, for a drawstring
- ❦ Washable fabric glue (or a needle and thread)
- ❦ Optional: Q-tip, safety pin

HOW TO DO IT

1. Turn the pillowcase inside out and cut along the closed side of the case. (How close to the edge you cut determines the length of the skirt, so for a longer skirt, cut close to the closed edge of the pillowcase, and for a shorter skirt, cut closer to the

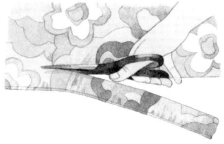

HOW TO MAKE A PILLOWCASE SKIRT

middle of the case.) The finished, open edge of the pillowcase will be the bottom of the skirt.

2. To create the casing (a tunnel of fabric) for your ribbon drawstring, fold the cut edge over about a half-inch all the way around and iron; then fold over another inch from there all the way around and iron that, too.

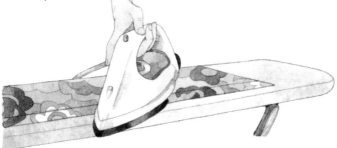

3. Lift the casing slightly and apply fabric glue along the half-inch underside edge; after the glue has been applied, press the glued edge back down with your fingers. (You may want to work in sections and use paper beneath the part you're working on to protect the rest of the pillowcase from getting glued together.) If you are using a needle and thread, in-

stead of gluing the edge down, sew a running stitch all the way around. (See our chapter on knots for an example.)

4. Let the glue dry and then turn the pillowcase right side out. Determine which side will be the front of your pillowcase skirt, and then put a tiny dab of fabric glue right in the middle, at the top, where your casing is. (Use a fingertip or a Q-tip for this, painting a very small amount of glue just on the surface of the fabric.)

5. Once that dab of glue dries, use your scissors to cut a small notch—just in the top layer of fabric—right there in the center of it. This is where the ends of your drawstring ribbon will poke out, and the gluing that you've done will help prevent the notch from fraying at the edges.

6. Take your ribbon and either make a small knot at the end or attach a safety pin to it, and begin to thread it through the casing. The bump created by the knot or safety pin makes it easier to find the end of the ribbon when it's inside the casing, which helps you know exactly how far you've pushed it through and how far you still have to go.

7. Once you've gotten your ribbon all the way through the casing, pull it through the notch, and untie the end or release the safety pin.

8. Pull on your skirt and tie the ribbon to secure it. Voila!

Playing Hopscotch

Believe it or not, hopscotch got its start not as a schoolyard game, but as a military exercise. During the early Roman Empire in ancient Britain, Roman soldiers ran through 100-foot long rectangular courses wearing full armor to help improve their footwork. Roman children drew up their own version of these courses, shortening the length and adding a scoring system, and the game of hopscotch was born.

The word *hopscotch* comes from hop, of course, meaning to jump, and *escocher,* an Old French word that means "to cut." The game as we know it dates back to at least 1801, and now hopscotch is played all over the world. In France, the game is called *Marelles.* Germans play *Tem-*

plehupfen, and kids in the Netherlands play *Hinkelbaan.* In Malaysia hopscotch is called *Ting-ting* or *Ketengteng,* and in India it's called *Ekaria Dukaria.* In Vietnam it's known as *Pico,* in Chile it's *Luche,* and in Argentina and many Spanish-speaking countries, it's called *Rayuela.*

COURTS

Make your own court using chalk on a sidewalk or driveway, or by using masking tape on a floor or carpet indoors.

Traditional American hopscotch courts look something like this:

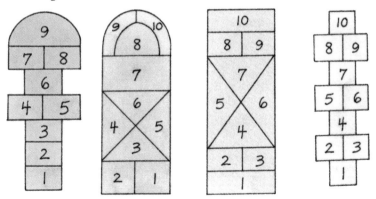

Super-old-fashioned courts had 6 boxes in a stack from 1 to 6, or 3 sets of 2 boxes:

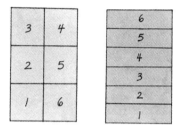

Fancier versions include the Monte Carlo and the Italian:

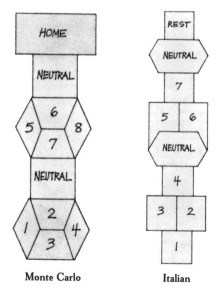

Monte Carlo   **Italian**

Or, you can always make up your own style of hopscotch court!

RULES

Nearly every girl knows the basic rules for hopscotch, but there are some interesting variations to liven things up.

In the most basic game, the first player stands behind the starting line to toss a marker (a rock, a penny, a beanbag, a button) in the first square. The marker must land in the correct square without bouncing out or touching a line. The player should hop over the first square to the second on one foot, then continue hopping all the way to the end of the court. Side-by-side squares can be straddled, with each foot on a square, but single squares must be hopped on with just one foot. A square with a marker in it must be hopped over, and any neutral, or safe, squares may be jumped through in any manner a player wishes.

When a player gets to the end of the court, she turns around and hops back through to the beginning, stopping to pick up her marker on the way back. If she makes it to the end without jumping on a line or putting two feet down in a square, she can continue her turn by throwing the marker into square number 2 and trying again. If a player steps on a line, misses a square, falls, or puts two feet down, her turn is over. When it's her turn again, she starts where she left off. The winner is the first player to complete one course of hopping up and back for every numbered square.

VARIATIONS

A French version of hopscotch is played on a spiral court and called, because of its shape, *Escargot* (snail) or *La Marelle Ronde* (round hopscotch). The court is drawn as a big snail or shell-like spiral and then sectioned into

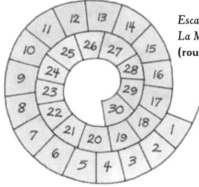

Escargot **(snail) or** *La Marelle Ronde* **(round hopscotch)**

squares, the number of which is limited only by the size of the spiral itself. In this version, each player hops on one foot to the center of the spiral and back out again. When a player is able to complete the full circuit, she can mark one square with her initials, and from then on she is allowed to have two feet in that square. The other players must hop over it. The game is over when all squares are marked (or if no one can reach the center), and the girl who wins is the one who has her initials in the most squares.

This variation, allowing the player to initial a square, can also be adapted for the traditional version of the game. After a player has completed one hopscotch sequence successfully, jumping all the way up and all the way back, she can throw her marker onto the court, and wherever the marker lands she can place her initials. Then that square is hers, and she is allowed to have two feet in it when hopping, while the other players must hop over it. In this version, each player is only allowed to initial one square per game.

A British variation, which can be used with traditional straight courts as well as with spiral courts, involves the player holding her marker between her feet and hopping from square to square on two feet without letting go of the marker or stepping on the lines.

In Toss-and-Reach Hopscotch, a player throws her marker into the center square, then hops to each square in order. From each square, she must reach in to pick up her marker without losing her balance or stepping on any lines.

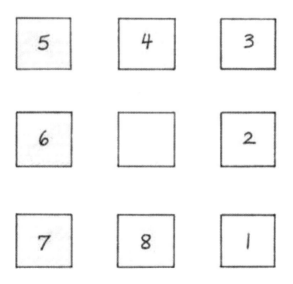

Toss-and-Reach Hopscotch

In Agility Hopscotch, the player must hop back and forth across the center line without touching any lines or losing her balance. She must hop on her left foot in squares marked L and on her right foot in squares marked R. She may rest with both feet down where the L and R are marked opposite each other.

Agility Hopscotch

Tracking Animals

The world is teeming with animals. Whether in the city or suburbs, your backyard or nearby woods, animals are everywhere, and you can find them—you just need to know where to look. Try the intersections of terrains: between a wooded area and a stream, or between a field and a stream. Animals need food, many need water, and they need cover, so look for thick spots of trees and brush or any place that an animal can hide from a predator, as well as trails and clearings they might use to get from shelter to food and back again.

HOW TO FIND AN ANIMAL

Option one: wait. Find a perch in a tree or on the ground. Animals will run when they sense movement, and repeated movement especially, so sit (or stand) and wait very, very silently for as long as it takes for an animal to come near. You might have a personal secret spot that you visit regularly, or a new place each time you go looking for deer, possum, or bear. In either case, breathe quietly and stay still. Let your ears hear as much as they can. Practice a wide angle of vision, where you scan left to right and right to left from the corners of your eyes without moving your head.

Option two: search for clues everywhere, from a bullfrog's loud croak to the delicate toe-print of a piping plover in the sand. The most noticeable clues are the tracks made by an animal's heel pad, claws, and inner and outer toes. Scan the ground for footprints, or for any indentations. Depending on how wet or dry the ground is, you may barely see the full footprint that shows up so well in light mud, snow, or sand.

Tracking guidebooks show pictures of each animal's front and hind prints, and they measure the print's size, and illustrate the track's patterns when the animal is walking slowly or bounding along. When you find a track, study it closely, measure, look for the next one to

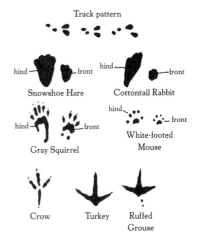

Track pattern

hind — front   hind — front
Snowshoe Hare   Cottontail Rabbit

hind —   hind
    — front   — front
Gray Squirrel   White-footed
                 Mouse

Crow   Turkey   Ruffed
                  Grouse

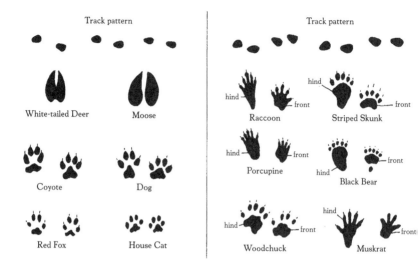

Track pattern

White-tailed Deer

Moose

Coyote

Dog

Red Fox

House Cat

Track pattern

Raccoon — hind, front

Striped Skunk — hind, front

Porcupine — hind, front

Black Bear — hind, front

Woodchuck — hind, front

Muskrat — hind, front

learn where the animal was headed, and, based on how far apart the tracks are, how fast they were trying to get there. If you are miles from the nearest animal track guide, remember or sketch the track the best you can and identify it later.

Admittedly, animal tracks can be hard to find. Unless it's been raining, or there's been snowmelt, or you're down by a creek, many footprints don't hold for long on forest floors, covered as they are with evergreen needles or decaying oak leaves. In such cases, seek out other signs of animal life. Listen for sounds of animals moving. Notice any bent grass, broken twigs, or tree scuffs and scratchings made by claws. These are signs that animals have been nearby, as are leaf bites and chews, or browse lines, where deer have eaten the leaves of a tree up to their standing height. Other intriguing animal signs are empty spots in otherwise vegetation-crowded places, packed-down trails and corridors where animals have traveled, small openings into larger brush, or bushes and small trees that have been crushed, squashed, or otherwise moved out of place. Follow all signs, and think like an animal wanting food and shelter, and you never know what you'll find.

WHEN YOU FIND AN ANIMAL

At last a porcupine or moose has come your way. What do you do? Freeze like there's no tomorrow. Those ears on the sides of an animal's heads are made for picking up the slightest movement and sound, and when they hear you, they'll run.

The stalk walk is the best way to move closer or to follow. Each time you lower a foot to the ground, land on the outside of the ball of your foot. Very lightly and very slowly roll onto the entire ball of your foot, feeling the ground beneath, and then decide whether to stay on the ball of your foot or let the whole foot touch the ground. Then and only then, in no hurry at all, slink your body weight forward to your front foot. The slower you walk, the quieter you can be, because leaves and twigs underfoot won't snap, they'll silently bend and mash. Try a super slow walk, where one step takes sixty seconds. (By the way, the stalk walk is great for any kind of spy activity.) You can bend your knees into a crouch to keep low, and even slide your arms to the ground for a stalking crawl (always landing on the outside of your knees and hands, and rolling in), and eventually working all the way down to the quietest belly crawl ever.

> **IF NO BEARS ARE OUT . . .**
>
> If you've had no luck finding any nonhuman animals, you can always play "Track the Bear" with your friends and practice your tracking skills. One person is the bear, or deer, or any animal you choose. She runs ahead with a several-minute head start and follows whatever path she chooses, for as long as she wants. Every few steps, the "bear" drops some beans (or some other non-polluting food). The trackers follow and collect the trail of beans till they find the "bear."

God's Eyes / Ojos de Dios

Ojos de Dios (oh-hoes day DEE-oes), or "God's Eyes," are yarn and stick creations traditionally made by the Huichol Indians. The Huichol, who live in the southern mountains of Mexico's Sierra Madre Occidental Range, call their God's eyes *sikuli,* which means "the power to see and understand things unknown." The design, created by yarn wrapped around the intersection of two sticks at right angles, forms the shape of a cross that is meant to symbolize the four elements: earth, air, fire, and water. When a child is born, a *sikuli* or *ojo de*

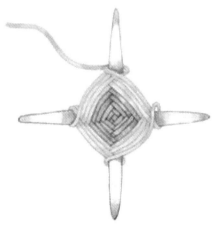

dios is made by the father; every year on the child's birth-day, another one is woven, until the child reaches the age of five. The *ojos de dios* are bound together and are kept throughout the person's life as a means of guaranteeing health and well being.

An *ojo de dios* can be as simple or complex as you like. Create one using different colored yarns; attach feathers or other decorations on the ends; or make two and com-bine them to form an eight-sided god's eye.

To make a basic four-sided *ojo de dios,* you'll need:

- ❖ Multi-colored yarn, or different colors of yarn

- ❖ 2 Popsicle sticks, or other sticks (chopsticks, wooden skewers that aren't sharp—you can even use toothpicks to make tiny ones)

- ❖ Glue

Take your base sticks and cross them over each other. If glue is handy, a small dab on the sticks helps to secure their intersection.

With your yarn, make a knot and tighten it where

the sticks intersect, to hold the cross shape. (Don't cut the yarn from the skein—you can cut it later, when you determine whether or not you'll be switching yarns or weaving until you reach the end of the sticks.) The knot should face the back side of your *ojo de dios*.

Wind the yarn in a figure eight around the intersection, up and down, then from left to right, to stabilize the sticks and cover the middle.

Once you have the intersection of the sticks covered and they are secure, weave the yarn by bringing it over a stick, then looping it around, and continuing the same over-around pattern on the other sticks.

You can continue in this pattern until you reach the end of the sticks. However, you may also mix things up by reversing the direction—if you're weaving in a clockwise pattern, switch to counterclockwise after a few rows, and vice versa. This provides a varied texture of recessed and raised rows.

If you wish to change yarn colors, make sure to tie the new yarn to the previous yarn so that the knot is on the back side of the god's eye. Clip off any excess yarn only at the end, when you're done.

When you are about a half-inch from the ends of the sticks, cut your yarn, leaving about 8 inches of yarn at the end. Tie a knot in the yarn close to the stick to end the weaving. You can use the "tail" of yarn to hang up the god's eye when you are done.

If you have feathers, bells, charms, or other decorations, you can glue or tie them to the four ends of the sticks.

❧

Tetherball

Tetherball requires a fast mind and equally fast hands to send the ball spiraling around the pole for a win. This was our favorite game growing up and we'd love to see more tetherball courts—and maybe someday tetherball as an Olympic event.

At its most basic, tetherball involves a ball—similar to a volleyball but somewhat squishier—tied to the top of a 10-foot pole by a rope. Two players try to hit the ball in one direction so that the rope winds completely around the pole. (But tetherball is also fun to play by yourself—in

your backyard when no one's around. You can practice and make up games for yourself, too. Like trying to duck before the ball hits you in the head.) Actual tetherball courts have a circle drawn on the ground around the pole and are divided in half. A drawn circle isn't necessary, but you should expect to need about 8-10 feet of space all around the pole, and each player should stay on her own side of the circle.

RULES

The rules of tetherball are deceptively simple: two people stand opposite each other, one person serves by hitting the ball in one direction around the pole, and the other tries to hit the ball in the opposite direction around the pole. The first player to get the rope wrapped completely around the pole is the winner.

Because the server has a big advantage (she gets to hit the ball first), players can decide to play matches instead of single games. The total number of games comprising the entire match is up to the players to decide, but the winner must win by at least two games. Another way to decrease the serving advantage is to have the player who doesn't serve choose which side of the circle she is on and which direction she is hitting.

Fouls and violations

How seriously you take fouls is something that needs to be decided before the game. Fouls include:

- Stepping across the center line.

- Server hitting the ball twice at the beginning before the opponent hits it once.

- Hitting the ball twice while it is still on your side of the circle.

- Hitting the ball with any part of the body other than the hand or forearm.

- Reaching around the pole and hitting the ball.

- Catching or holding the ball.

- Throwing the ball.

- Touching the pole with any part of your body.

- Hitting the rope with any part of your body.

If you only have a few players, you can treat these fouls as mere violations and resume the game by stopping the ball and returning it to where it was wrapped when the violation occurred. The non-violating player gets to serve, and then either player can hit the ball. If a player racks up three violations, the opponent automatically wins.

If the two players commit a violation at the same time, they must do a pole drop to start the game again. Both players hold the ball with one hand, lifting it about three feet away from the pole, directly over the line dividing their two halves of the circle, and then let go of the ball at the same time. The ball should hit the pole, and then either player can hit it to continue the game.

No matter how you decide to play, the only absolute game-ender is grabbing the pole. If a player does that, she immediately loses the game.

EQUIPMENT

The Ball

A tetherball is the only piece of equipment that you must purchase specifically for the game and is similar to a volleyball, but softer. It will have either a loop sticking out of the surface or a recessed spot on the surface of the ball to attach the rope.

The Pole

The best pole for the job is a 10 to 12-foot long, 2-inch diameter steel pipe sunk 2 feet into the ground, with an eyebolt run through the pole about 4 inches from the top for attaching the rope. This may be a good time to take a field trip to your local hardware or plumbing supply store. But with a good eye you might be able to spot a likely pole around town that will serve nicely for the game. Just remember to untie the ball and take it home with you when you are done.

MAKING A TETHERBALL COURT IN YOUR YARD

Here's your shopping list:

- Steel pipe, 10 to 12 feet long, 2″ diameter
- Steel pipe, 2 feet long, slightly wider than 2″ diameter
- Eyebolt with nut (for attaching the rope to the top of the pole)
- Drill and bit capable of drilling through metal
- Concrete mix
- Tetherball
- Rope (if not included with the tetherball)

Making the Court

Drill a hole through the pole about 4 inches from the top for the eyebolt, and put the eyebolt in place.

Dig a hole in your lawn, gravel driveway, or backyard about 2½ feet deep, with a 2-foot diameter.

Pour in 6 inches of concrete and let it set for at least 30 minutes.

Stand the 2-foot long pipe in the center of the hole and add concrete around the pipe to fill the hole (it's a good idea to have something to keep the pipe in place while the surrounding concrete sets; also, the pipe should be level with the ground and should protrude just above ground level, but not so much that it sticks up enough to get nicked by a lawn mower).

Once the concrete is fully set, slide the large pole into your concrete-and-pole base (this should be a solid, tight fit, but the long pole is removable).

Attach the rope and ball.

&

Make a Homemade Geyser

If you've ever had a hankering for making a 12-foot geyser in your backyard, but weren't sure how to do it, worry no more. Below is all you need to know to make your very own homemade soda fountain.

You will need:

- 1 roll of mint-flavored Mentos candy
- 1 two-liter bottle of warm diet soda
- Goggles
- 1 piece of paper

HOW YOU DO IT

1. Find a wide open space outdoors, like a big back-yard.

2. Place the warm (at least room-temperature) bottle of soda on the ground. Make sure it's on a stable, flat surface so that it doesn't tip over.

3. This is the tricky part: to make the geyser work,

you're going to need to drop the candies into the diet soda all at once, which takes a certain amount of finesse and preparation. There are a few ways to do this. You can open one end of the Mentos roll and try to push the candies out from the top, but that may be slow-going (you want all of the candies in the soda as quickly as possible). Another way is to unwrap the Mentos and then roll up a piece of paper into a tube (just slightly bigger than the candy roll and no bigger than the opening of the soda bottle) to hold the candies and make it easier to pour them in all at once.

4. BEFORE YOU DROP THE MENTOS INTO THE BOTTLE, put on your goggles and warn your friends to stand back.

5. Open the bottle, and then quickly put your paper tube of Mentos just above the mouth of the soda bottle to let the candies fall in—and then quickly move out of the way to avoid getting sprayed.

6. Watch what happens!

WHY IT WORKS

Even the originators of the Mentos-and-diet-soda geyser admit that there is a lot of debate over exactly how and why this experiment works. What everyone can agree on, though, is that it's a lot of fun.

One of the main characteristics of soda is its fizzy and bubbly nature, which comes from the carbon dioxide gas added to it in the bottling process (hence the term "carbonated beverage"). If you've ever tasted "flat" soda, you'll know how important that gas is to a soda's flavor and taste, and if you've ever opened a bottle of soda that's been shaken, you know how that carbon dioxide gas makes soda behave when it's been knocked around a little.

When a soda bottle is closed, the carbon dioxide gas is trapped in the liquid, surrounded by water molecules that prevent it from expanding to form bubbles (this is called "surface tension"). But once you open the bottle, the surface tension is broken: the gas mixes with air and creates the foamy, bubbly stuff you see when you pour yourself a glass (and the sound you hear when you open the bottle in the first place). Dropping anything into a glass of soda disrupts the surface tension—drop a penny

in a glass of soda and you'll see how the coin immediately becomes covered in bubbles—but dropping Mentos in there is another story.

It turns out that the surface of the mint-flavored Mentos candies is covered with thousands of tiny indentations, and all those nooks and crannies (called "nucleation sites") give the carbon dioxide gas something to grab onto—some room, essentially, to break free of the water molecules around it and expand. (The fruit-flavored Mentos candies actually have a smooth, waxy coating, which is why mint-flavored is the way to go in terms of geyser-making.) If you were able to watch your homemade geyser happen in slow motion, you would see bubbles forming all over the candies as soon as they drop into the soda (and continuing to form as the candies sink in the liquid). This sudden release of carbon dioxide gas makes the soda bubble over dramatically—and because the Mentos go straight to the bottom of the bottle, due to their weight, and because the top of the bottle is narrow, there's nowhere for those bubbles to go but straight up and out of the bottle, shooting anywhere from 12 to 30 feet in the air.

Now for the big question: Why diet soda instead of regular soda? For whatever reason, perhaps because it is made with chemical sugar substitutes, diet soda makes for bigger geysers—and a less sticky cleanup! (Also, since the diet soda has no sugar content, it doesn't draw bugs, which is definitely something to consider when you're working outside.)

⤶

The Three Sisters

The Three Sisters aren't actually real girls, but they support one another, as sisters should. So named by the innovative Iroquois (the Native American tribe also called the Haudenosaunee), the Three Sisters are corn, beans, and squash.

The Iroquois discovered that, when grown together, these three plants make each other stronger. The sturdy corn stalks double as poles and support the beans. The squash's floppy, oversized leaves perfectly mulch the ground and keep the weeds at bay. This vegetable garden combination has been a North American tradition for centuries. You can try it in your backyard.

GETTING PREPARED

Before planting your seeds of corn, bean and squash (and for the last, feel free to substitute pumpkin), there are three basic strategies you need to know.

1. Nurture Healthy Soil

As the old saying goes, dirt's beneath your fingernails, soil's under your feet. The truth about gardening is that it's all about preparing good soil, with fertile proportions of water, air, and compost. Humus and manure also add nutrients to your soil, as will the mulch you place on top. Pile on leaves and other garden debris; they will decay in the soil and nourish it from within.

How do you know if soil is healthy? Good soil is something you can feel. It crumbles airily between your fingers and has worms in it.

2. Experiment with Compost

Gardeners wax eloquent about compost. And you should hear them talk about compost tea, which is when you mix compost and water and sprinkle it over your plants as fertilizer. You can purchase bags of prepared compost at your local nursery.

Compost is also a backyard project, called "a simple heap of green and brown." Green is kitchen scraps—but never meat! Brown is fallen leaves, pine tree needles, and even newspapers, cut into strips. Toss it all together, add water every few days, and turn over with a pitchfork once in a while.

In a few months, the natural process of decay turns this heap to compost, full of vitamins for your plants. Add some to your garden soil. (It must be admitted that despite gardeners' eloquence, sometimes mulch piles don't work. If this happens to you, it's okay.)

3. Know the Date of Last Frost

Many seeds should not be planted outdoors until after the date of the last frost, and this includes corn, beans, and squash (others, like lettuce and peas, are cold-weather crops and can be planted in mid-spring). The best way to find this magic date is to ask any seasoned gardener in your neighborhood. This is called "talking over the fence," and is without a doubt the best way to learn how to garden.

PLANTING YOUR SISTERS

Now: You are ready, your soil is dark and crumbly and filled with compost, and the last frost is a distant memory. To plant the Three Sisters, prepare a garden spot three to five feet in diameter, and mound the soil up about one foot.

In the center of the mound make five holes, each an inch deep, and plant two corn seeds in each hole.

In two weeks: The corn seedlings will emerge. Prune the smaller, weaker one from each hole; five corn stalks will remain in the mound. (This two-seed planting trick can be used every time you plant; it's the best way to find the seeds most likely to succeed.) Then plant the bean seeds in seven holes in a circle around the corn, planting two seeds in each hole, knowing you'll prune the weaker ones later.

Two weeks after that: The beans will sprout. Once again, prune the smaller ones.

One week later: The beans should be tall enough to start winding through the growing corn stalks; help them find their way. Then plant the seeds for squash or pumpkin in eleven holes around the corn, repeating the two-seed method you now know well.

All summer long: Water very well each day.

In the fall: You'll have a feast of corn, beans, and squash (or pumpkins) that would make the Iroquois—and your sisters—proud.

Friendship Bracelets

Friendship bracelets can be very simple or extremely intricate, but at heart they're just colorful embroidery floss woven into lovely patterns, to be given to dear friends. Originally part of Native American life, particularly in Central America, these handwoven bracelets became popular in the United States in the 1970s—and not just for girls. President Bill Clinton sported one in the first televised interview of his post-presidential years.

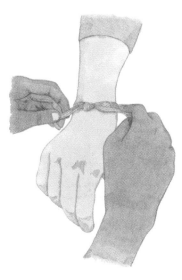

FRIENDSHIP BRACELETS

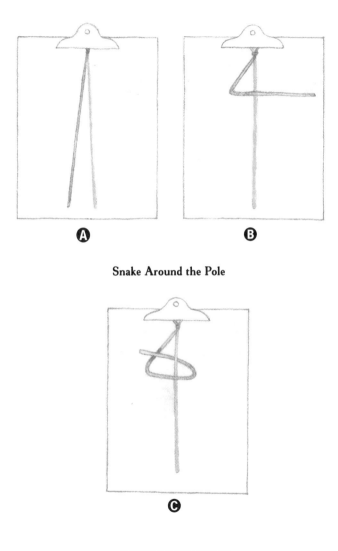

A

B

Snake Around the Pole

C

The slender **Snake Around the Pole** is the easiest bracelet to make.

1. Cut two strands from different colors of embroidery floss, using a bit less than one yard.

2. Hold the two strands together. Tie a knot at one end, leaving 2 inches above the knot. Use a safety pin to attach it to your pants or the arm of a sofa (if you do that, make sure your parents won't mind a tiny hole). Some people use tape, but it can come off and mess up the pattern. You can also use a clipboard, putting the knot just under the clamp **Ⓐ**.

3. Separate the two strands. Take the left and cross it on top of the right, making the shape of a number 4 **Ⓑ**. Then loop the left strand under the right and bring it through the opening created by the "4" shape **Ⓒ**.

4. This forms a knot that you will pull tight by sliding it toward the big knot at the top. Repeat

this with the same string for as long as you want this color. When you're ready to change colors, just take the right-hand strand and move it to the left.

5. With this new left-hand strand of the second color, repeat steps 3 and 4 until you're ready to switch colors again, or until you're done with the bracelet.

6. Finish with another big knot, and leave enough room to tie the bracelet around your friend's wrist.

For a heftier and more colorful **Snake Around the Pole,** use four colors, with two strands of each color. Knot the strands together, and attach to a hard surface. Follow the directions for the first Snake Around the Pole, but twist the knot around seven other strings instead of only one. Tighten each knot by pulling it toward the top. Repeat for as long as you want that color, then switch to the next. Continue until you're done. Knot to finish.

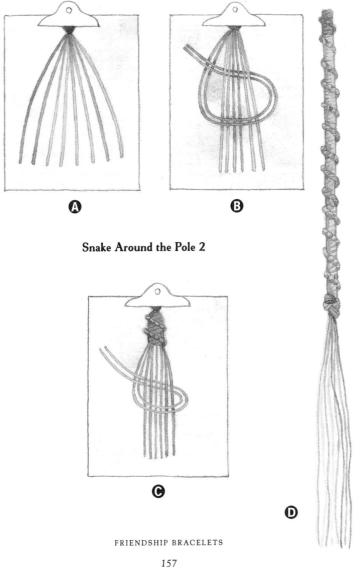

Snake Around the Pole 2

The flatter, wider **Candy Stripe** is a different kind of knot bracelet. With the string on the left, you'll tie a knot around each strand one at a time, moving to the right. All this knotting can be a bit tedious—which shows your true devotion to the friend who gets the bracelet! Once you get the hang of it, though, you can knot a friendship bracelet practically without looking.

1. Cut three strands each of three colors, about one yard long. Tie a knot at the top, leaving two inches above the knot. Attach the strands to a hard surface, like a clipboard, or use a safety pin to attach it to your pants. Separate the strands by color **A**.

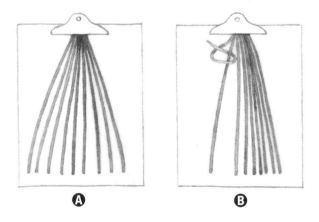

A   **B**

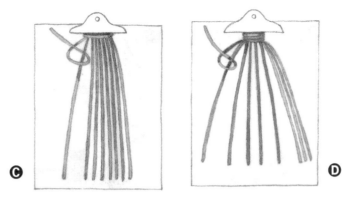

2. Start with the leftmost strand and make the "4" shape over top of the strand directly to its right. Bring the left strand back through the opening created by the "4" shape, and slide it to the top, pulling the knot tight **B**. Repeat for each of the other strands, moving left to right, always using the leftmost strand to make the knot. When all eight knots are done, the strand will be at the far right, where it should stay.

3. Take the strand that is now the leftmost **C**, and start knotting across the strands, as in step 2. As before, when it reaches the far right, let it rest, and allow the new leftmost strand to make a new row of knots **D**. The key to success is to make sure you

make all the knots very tight, and push each finished row tightly to the top.

4. Repeat the process until you are done. Leave room at the end, tie a knot, and then fasten it with care onto a friend's ankle or wrist.

Candy Stripe

Tree Swing

What you need:

- Wood, 2 x 8 inches and 2 feet long
- Rope
- Two eyebolts, 8″ long, with a ³⁄₈″ thread, two nuts and four washers
- A tennis ball, a sock, and some twine
- Drill with ³⁄₈″ bit

The hardest part of building a tree swing is finding a well-suited branch. We can tell you that a tree-swing branch should be at least 8 inches in diameter, but on a tree tall enough for a swing, that can be difficult to measure precisely. You'll also need a strong rope long enough to get around the branch and down to the ground and back up again.

Your swing should not be on a white birch, because those rubbery branches readily bend. Look for a hardy oak or maple. The spot on the branch where you hang your swing should be far enough from the trunk so no

one is hurt when they swing, but close enough so the branch is still strong.

The second hardest part is getting the rope up and over the branch. To forestall several hours of standing with a rope and squinting into the sun, we have a strategy to suggest:

❦ Put a tennis ball in an old sock. Wrap twine around the sock and make a knot so the tennis ball stays put, and make sure you have enough twine on the skein so it can unfurl the length up to the tree branch, and back down again.

❦ Stand under the tree and aim the tennis-ball-in-the-sock over the branch. It may take a few tries, but it is much easier than just flinging the rope up to the branch.

❦ Once up and over, the tennis ball sock will land near your feet, trailed by a long strand of twine. Knot the twine to the rope to be used in the tree swing. (Try a sheetbend knot, it's designed to join different sized-ropes.) Pull the twine until the rope is over the branch. You might want to toss the ball/rope combo over again, to double-loop the rope over the branch. When all is in place, detach the twine. The rope is set.

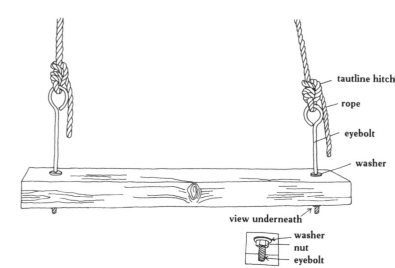

tautline hitch
rope
eyebolt
washer

view underneath

washer
nut
eyebolt

The easiest part is making the seat and procuring a long length of rope. Find or cut a 2-foot long piece of 2-by-8 wood. Draw a line down the center, lengthwise, and measure 2 inches in from either side. That's where to drill the two holes. Put an eyebolt through each hole, with a washer above the wood and a washer and nut below it. Knot the two ends of the rope to the eyes of the eyebolt (a tautline hitch is handy here).

If you don't want to use the bolts, you can push the ropes themselves through the holes and tie with strong stopper knots. Either way, check underneath every so often and tighten the bolts or knots.

Making a Peg Board Game

Perfect for car trips or rainy days, this ancient logic game is surprisingly easy to make but difficult to master. Traditionally, it is a triangular board with fourteen pegs and fifteen holes. The goal is to jump one peg over another until only one remains.

Needed:

- 1 flat board of wood, $6'' \times 6''$ (at least one inch thick is a good size). Any shape is fine; it doesn't have to be triangular.
- 14 fluted dowel pins, $\frac{5}{16}'' \times 1\frac{1}{2}''$. Available at any hardware store.
- Ruler
- Power drill, with a $\frac{5}{16}''$ bit.

Make a dot at the top of the board for your starting point. Lightly draw one diagonal line and then another, marking your triangle on the wood. In addition to the top dot, mark four dots down one side of the triangle, four along the other side, and three dots along the bottom.

Draw dots for the middle holes, too. Use your ruler so everything lines up.

Drill a ½″ hole right where you have drawn each dot. Some people measure ½ inch up the drill bit and put some masking tape on that spot so they can easily gauge the hole, although once you do enough of these, you'll get the feel of it. Test each hole with a dowel, making sure the dowel easily moves in and out. When all fifteen holes are done, shake out the sawdust, and you're ready to play.

MAKING A PEG BOARD GAME

Rules of the Game: Darts

D arts is a game with a long history. It's thought to have been invented by soldiers throwing arrows at the bottom of tree trunks or wooden casks. Modern dart boards are most commonly made of boar bristles or sisal fibers (or, in the case of Velcro dart games, felt). Playing darts takes some practice, and some math skills, but mostly it's just fun to throw something across the room. Make sure you give annoying siblings and small animals a wide berth.

SETTING UP THE BOARD

A regulation board has a diameter of 18 inches and is divided by thin metal wire into 22 sections. Make sure to mount your dart board so that the center of the double bull (the bull's-eye) is 5 feet 8 inches from the floor. Mark the toeline, called the oche (pronounced to rhyme with "hockey"), 7 feet, 9¼ inches from the face of the board.

BASIC RULES

To determine shooting order, each player shoots for the bull's-eye. The one who comes closest gets to go first.

Each turn consists of three darts, which must be thrown from behind the oche. For a throw to count, the point of the dart must touch the board. If a dart bounces off the board or misses it completely, it does not get a score (and also can't be rethrown).

SCORING

The dart board is divided into wedges, with point values marked along the outer edge of the circle. Two rings overlap the playing area; landing outside these rings scores a player face-value points for that area of the board. Landing between the first inner ring and the second inner ring scores a player double the points for that section. Landing between the second inner ring and the bull's-eye earns triple points. Hitting outside the outer wire scores nothing.

HOW TO THROW

First, aim. Look at the target you want to hit. Lift your arm up, bent at the elbow so that the sharp end of the dart faces the dartboard. The dart should be tipped slightly up. Check your aim and line up the dart with your sight line. Move the hand holding the dart back toward your body, then pitch the dart forward, releasing the dart and making sure to follow through with your arm. The optimal follow-through will end with your hand pointing at the target (not having your hand fall to your side). When throwing, try not to move your body—the throwing action should come from your shoulder.

PLAYING THE GAME: THE 301

The object of this game, which is most commonly played by two people, is to start with a score of 301 and count down to exactly zero. Each player has a three-throw turn, and the point value of their hits is subtracted from 301. A player can only start subtracting once they "double"— that is, hit one of the doubles on the board. Once that is accomplished, the scores will begin to count. If the total score of the three throws exceeds the remaining score for that player, the score returns to what it was at the start of the turn. A double must be hit to end the game.

PLAYING THE GAME: ROUND THE CLOCK

In this game, players take turns trying to hit each number, from 1 to 20. Each player has a three-throw turn; players advance to the next number on the board by hitting each number in order. The first person to get to 20 wins.

PLAYING THE GAME: CRICKET

This strategy game is typically played with two players, or two teams of two players each. To win at Cricket, a player must "close" the numbers 15 to 20 and the bull's-eye before any other player, and must also have the highest point count. "Closing" a number means hitting it three times in one or more turns (hitting a single closes a number in three throws; hitting a double and then a single closes a number in two throws; and hitting a triple closes a number in a single throw). You don't have to close numbers in any particular order—but you do want to close them before the other players.

To keep track of the score, you'll need a scoreboard (a blackboard on the wall or a pen and pad of paper will work). Write out the numbers vertically for each player, from 20 down to 15, then "B" for bull's-eye. Each player's turn consists of three throws, and only darts that land in the numbers 15-20 or in the bull's-eye count. (You don't get points for hitting numbers 1-14.) Points start to accumulate once a number is closed, and are tallied as follows: the center of the bull's-eye is worth 50 points and the outer ring of the bull's-eye gets 25; numbers 15-20 are worth their face value, but landing in the doubles ring doubles the number's value, and landing in the triple ring (the inner ring between the doubles ring and the bull's-eye) triples it.

When a player hits a number once, you put a slash (/) by the number. When that number is hit a second time by a player, you turn the slash into an X. When that number is "closed," or hit a third time, you draw a circle around the X. Once a number has been closed, if any player hits it, the points for that number go to the player who originally closed it. Once a number has been closed by all the players, no points are awarded for that number for the rest of the game. Total up the points after one player closes all her numbers plus the bull's-eye, and the person or team with the highest number of points is the winner.

DART LINGO

Arrows: Darts

Bust: Hitting a number higher than you need to go out

Chucker: Indifferent thrower

Clock: Dartboard

Double In: Starting a game with a double

Double Out: Winning a game on a double

Hat Trick: Three bull's-eyes

Leg: One game of a match

Slop: Hitting a number other than the intended

Trombones: A total turn score of 76 points

Wet Feet: Standing with your feet over the line

Bird Watching

ird watching might seem difficult (or even boring), but we can assure you, it is not. Birds are everywhere—easy to spot and fun to observe. Most birders keep a life-list journal, a kind of bird diary, by writing down the birds they see. As you begin to bird, you can use a small spiral notebook to make a life-list journal for yourself, writing down the names of the birds you find, or sketching their distinguishing features so you can look them up in a bird identification book once you're back home. All you need to go bird watching is a pair of binoculars, a good bird guidebook, comfortable clothes, your life-list journal—and some patience. Bird watching demands a certain kind of presence on the part of the birder: You must become a part of nature rather than stand outside of it. Here are eight common birds to start you off on a lifetime pursuit of bird watching.

AMERICAN ROBIN

The American Robin is one of the most popular species of birds, a regular visitor to front porches and in backyards. The Robin can be seen throughout North Amer-

ica and is recognizable by its gray head, orange underbelly (usually brighter in the male), and distinctive crescents around the eyes. During breeding season, adult males grow eye-catching black feathers on their heads; after the season is over, the plumes fall out (just like their middle-aged male human counterparts). The Robin's song sounds like a whistled musical phrase, sometimes described as "cheerily, cheer up, cheer up."

Cool facts:
The American Robin is the state bird of Connecticut, Michigan, and Wisconsin. And there is a Crayola crayon color named after the color of the eggs: Robin's Egg Blue.

BLUE JAY

The Blue Jay, a large crested songbird, is immediately recognizable by its characteristic bold blue coloring. Blue Jays are intelligent, resourceful, and adaptable. They can imitate the sounds of hawks, driving off competitors for their food, and have a reputation for stealing the eggs and nests of smaller birds during breeding season.

Cool facts:
Male and female Blue Jays look the same. Blue Jays living in captivity have shown themselves to be capable of using tools, grabbing strips of newspaper to rake in food pellets just outside their cages.

CHICKADEE

There are five species of Chickadee in North America: the most common, the Black-Capped Chickadee, is found all over North America; the Carolina  Chickadee is found in the southeast; the Mountain Chickadee is found in the Rockies; the Chestnut-Backed Chickadee is found along the Pacific coast; and the Mexican Chickadee is found in Arizona, New Mexico, and west and central Mexico. Chickadees are smaller than sparrows and very acrobatic. The Chickadee has two characteristic calls: one that sounds like "cheeeeeese bur-gers" and one that gives them their name: "chick-a-dee-dee-dee-dee."

Cool facts:
The Black-Capped Chickadee hides seeds for later, and can remember thousands of hiding places. The bird's seemingly simple calls are actually used to communicate sometimes complex information, such as identity or predator alerts, to other Chickadees.

RUBY-THROATED HUMMINGBIRD

These tiny birds are the only species of humming-bird that breeds in eastern North America and are present as far north as New Brunswick, Canada. The birds hover at flow-ers, and their name derives from the humming sound emanating from their wings.

In the winter, the Ruby-Throated Hummingbird flies nonstop across the Gulf of Mexico to Central America. To fuel themselves for the journey, they eat so much that they double their body mass in the days before they leave. The Ruby-Throated Hummingbird has an iridescent green back; the males have a bright red throat and the females have a white throat. The female is also larger than the male.

Cool facts:
The Ruby-Throated Hummingbird beats its wings 53 times per second. Also, its legs are so short that is cannot walk or hop, only shuffle. But it manages to scratch its head by lifting its foot up and over its wing.

RED-TAILED HAWK

The Red-tailed Hawk is roughly the size of a small cat (22 inches long and 2 to 4 pounds). Categorized as raptors—birds of prey— they are meat eaters, or carnivores. They have hooked beaks; their feet have three toes pointed forward and one turned back; and their claws, or talons, are long, curved and very sharp. They can live as long as twenty-one years, though the more typical lifespan is about ten years. This variety of hawk is found throughout North America, from central Alaska and northern Canada to the mountains of Panama. It has a rasping scream that is most commonly voiced while soaring.

Cool facts:
A Red-Tailed Hawk's eyesight is eight times as powerful as a human's. A hawk kills its prey using its long talons; if the prey is too large to swallow whole, the hawk rips it into smaller pieces with its beak.

MALLARD

The Mallard duck is found throughout North America and all across Eurasia, most noticeably in urban park

 ponds. It is the ancestor of almost all domestic duck breeds. Male Mallards have iridescent green heads,

reddish chests, and gray bodies; the female is a mottled brown.

Cool facts:
Mallards are monogamous and pair up long before the spring breeding season. The males are loyal, but only the female incubates the eggs and takes care of the duck-lings.

RED-BREASTED SAPSUCKER

The Red-Breasted Sapsucker is common in the forests of the west coast, but rarely seen in the east. They are rec-ognizable by their markings: red heads and breasts, and a prominent white stripe across black wings. Male and female Red-Breasted Sapsuckers look alike; younger birds are mot-tled brown but have white wing-stripes, just like the adults. These birds get their name from the way they eat: foraging for food by drill-ing horizontal rows of holes in tree trunks and later feeding on the sap and the insects drawn to it.

Cool facts:

Hummingbirds often make use of sapsucker feeding holes, nesting near them and following the sapsucker around during the day to feed at the sap wells it keeps active.

AMERICAN TREE SPARROW

The American Tree Sparrow is actually not closely associated with trees, as it forages and nests on the ground. It is a common "backyard bird" found throughout southern Canada and the northern United States. The American

Tree Sparrow is a small songbird, only 6 inches long, with a brown crown and eyestripe against a grey head, and a dark spot in the center of its breast.

Cool facts:

In the summer months, the American Tree Sparrow eats only insects. In the winter it only eats seeds and other plant foods.

Washing the Car

Summer is a perfect time to run your own car wash. Here's how to do it with baking soda and vinegar.

Before you start washing, sprinkle baking soda through the car's interior to remove odors. Vacuum it up when the outside washing is done.

For the car body, grab a bucket, and pour in ½ cup of vinegar for every gallon of water; scrub car with a big sponge.

For windows, mirrors, and interior plastic, mix 2 cups of water and ½ cup vinegar in an empty spray bottle. You can add up to ¼ cup of rubbing alcohol and, to make it look fancier, one drop each, no more, of blue and green food coloring. Instead of rags, use newspapers to clean and shine windows.

❧

Make a Sit-Upon

The Sit-Upon is a homemade waterproof cushion that makes the perfect seat for around the campfire, near a tent, your backyard, a sporting event, or any use you can imagine.

THE VERY SIMPLE SIT-UPON

Needed:

* Plastic bags, the kind from the grocery store, about 12 inches by 12 inches with the handles cut off. Can be larger if you wish; any size bag will work.

* Lots of newspaper for the padding. The more, the comfier; try a pile 1½ to 2 inches high.

* Duct tape, or other strong and wide packing tape.

Stack the newspapers neatly. Cut or fold them to fit inside the plastic bag. Place them in the bag. Squeeze

the air from the bag and fold it tightly around the newspaper. Use a second bag if necessary, to catch the other side of the newspaper stack. Tape all sides of the bag to keep out water and debris.

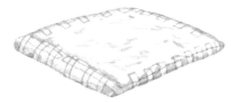

THE FANCIER SIT-UPON

Like most everything, a Sit-Upon can be made fancier and more decorative. The newspapers in the plastic bag can be covered with a waterproof cover.

Needed:

❖ The Very Simple Sit-Upon, as on previous page.

❖ Pieces of old wallpaper make an excellent cover, as do squares cut from a vinyl tablecloth, oilcloth, or a shower curtain. Be as creative as you'd like; the only guideline is that the material should be as waterproof, or water-resistant, as possible. Cut into 15 by 15 inch squares. If you prefer an even larger sit-upon, choose any measurement, cutting the squares 1½–2 inches larger on each side than the newspaper-and-plastic sit-upon that will fit inside.

❖ A hole punch.

❖ Cord, twine, lanyard, or other strong string, measuring six or seven times the length of one side of the cover.

To Construct:

Cut the square covers to size. Punch holes every inch or so around all four edges of the covers, doing both at the same time, so the holes match up. Then place the Very Simple Sit-Upon between the two covers. To sew, string the cord through the holes using an overcast stitch (start on top, enter the hole, pull the cord through and out to the side, take it over to the top, and then sew in from the top of the next hole.) If needed, wrap tape around the end of the string to stiffen it and make it easier to sew. Leave extra cord at start and finish for the square knot at the end.

MAKE A SIT-UPON

THE SIT-UPON TRAVELER'S EDITION

You might be taking your Sit-Upon with you on a hike, or someplace where it would be handy not to have to hold it while you walk.

To make the fanny-pack carrier, procure a belt or rope that is long enough to tie around your waist. Before you sew the edges of the Sit-Upon, lay the rope or belt along one side. Stitch the rope or belt to the Sit-Upon as you sew that side of the cover. When you tie on the belt, the Sit-Upon will lay behind you as you walk.

For the messenger-bag alternative, attach an even longer piece of rope that will go over your head and over one shoulder, messenger-bag style, with the Sit-Upon resting across your back.

Lemon-Powered Clock

A pair of lemons and a quick trip to the hardware store is all you need to convert natural chemical energy into electric power.

Alessandro Volta invented the battery in Italy, in 1800, combining zinc, copper, and an acid to create energy. A common lemon can provide the acid (you can also use a potato if there's no lemon around), and you can rig one to run your own digital clock.

What you need:

♦ A battery operated digital clock without a plug. It can use two AA batteries, or a round battery. Depending on the connections, you have to rig the wires in different ways, but that's where the fun starts.

♦ Two fairly large galvanized nails. Nails are measured in length (in inches) and in diameter (with designations of 3d, 6d, 8d, 10d, and the like). We used a 16d, 3½ inches—a solid nail. Galvanized nails are a must and we'll explain why below.

◆ Copper wire. Uncoated wire is easier. If your wire comes with a coating, use a wire stripper to remove an inch or two of the covering.

◆ Three electrician's clips.

◆ Two lemons, or one very large lemon cut in half.

WHAT YOU DO

In five simple steps, here is how you run a digital clock on a lemon.

Step One: Place the lemons on a plate, or any flat surface that can serve as the base for the clock. Push one nail into each lemon and then, as far away from the nails as possible, also push in a strand of copper wire. Label your lemons one and two. What you're going to do now is create a closed circuit, so energy can flow from the lemon into the clock and back again.

Step Two: Open up the clock's battery compartment. Depending on your clock, there are two AA batteries, or a single battery that looks like a button. Remove the battery (you'll be replacing its energy, believe it or not, with the lemon-nail-and-copper concoction you've just created). Notice that the positive and negative points are marked as such.

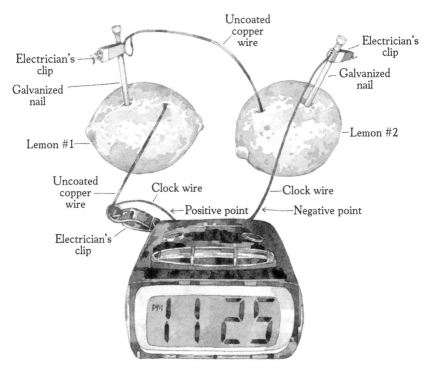

Step Three: On lemon number one, use the electrician's clip to connect the copper wire to the positive point in the clock. This may be a challenge; in some cases it is easier said than done.

If you can't connect your wire to the positive point in the battery compartment, you'll need to remove the clock's plastic backing and open up the clock. An adult should help with this, and remember, once you take the clock apart it may not go back together. Inside, you'll see that the positive and negative points are connected to wires on the inside of the clock. You can remove the wires from the back of the battery compartment, and then use them to make your connections. If you have a two-AA-battery clock, and inside you find two positive wires, make sure you connect your copper wire with both. Once you've figured this out, the rest is a breeze.

Step Four: On lemon number two, connect the nail to the clock's negative point. You may need to move the lemon into a new position so you can clip the nail to the clock.

Step Five: Link the copper wire from lemon number two to the nail sticking out of lemon number one. You'll see now that you've made an entire electrical circuit, from clock, to lemon, to the next lemon, and back to the clock. If all has gone well, the clock now works, because just under one volt of electricity is coursing the circuit.

If the clock does not work, make sure all connections are secure, and then double-check the directions. If several months from now the clock stops, replace the lemons, or the nails, and it should begin ticking once again.

WHY IT WORKS

The nail has been galvanized, which means it was coated with zinc to help resist rust. The lemon contains acid. This acid dissolves the zinc on the nail. In chemistry terms, this means that the zinc loses an electron and becomes a positive force. The moisture in the lemon functions as an electrolyte, a fluid that conducts electrons—if you will, a swimming pool for electrons.

The electron shoots out of the zinc, through the lemon, to react with the copper on the wire. The copper gains an electron and becomes a negative force. The exchange of electrons is a chemical reaction. It creates chemical energy, or charge. All that charge needs is a circuit.

The electron exchange buzzes around the circuit you built—zinc/nail to copper wire to clock to copper wire to nail to lemon to copper to zinc/nail to lemon, and so on. That's the transfer from chemical energy to electricity, and it gets the clock going as well as any manufactured battery.

Daisy Chains and Ivy Crowns

To make a daisy chain, pick twenty or so daisies. Near the bottom of the stem, but not too close, slit a slender lengthwise hole with your fingernail. Thread the next daisy through this hole until the flower head rests on the first stem. Take care not to pull too hard; daisy chains are lovely, but fragile. If you want to see lots of stem between the daisies, make the slit farther from the blossom. If you prefer a tightly packed garland, slit closer to the flower itself, and pinch off the rest of the stem. Continue until the daisy chain seems long enough fit around the top of your head. To

finish, tangle the last stem around the first daisy, and tie it off with a longish piece of grass. Put the chain of daisies on your head, close your eyes, and make a wish. You can also make them into a necklace, or preserve them by leaving them to dry in the back of a dark closet shelf.

In ancient Greece and Rome, circles of ivy, laurel, and olive branches crowned the victories of athletes and marked as excellent the pursuits of scholars, artists, and soldiers. As the ancient Greek  playwright Euripedes wrote in *The Bacchantes*: "Come, let us crown your head with ivy."

Ivy crowns are incredibly simple to make, too. Ivy has large leaves and long, thick stems. Start with a piece of ivy many times the circumference of your head. Mark off the size you want and then start twining the ivy around itself, until the crown is full. Tuck the end under and don your new headpiece.

DAISY CHAINS AND IVY CROWNS

How to Be a Spy

The word "spy" comes to us from ancient words meaning "to look at or watch." And indeed, despite the modern movie emphasis on technology and machines as integral to a spy's bag of tricks, in essence what makes an excellent spy is her ability to watch, pay attention, look, and learn.

TOP-SECRET COMMUNICATION

SECRET CODES

A code is a way to send a message while keeping it a secret from someone who isn't supposed to know about it. Codes can be easy or complicated—the trick is to make sure the person on the receiving end of your secret message has the key to decode it without making it too easy for anyone else to crack. Here are a few simple codes you can use.

- Write each word backwards
- Read every second letter
- Use numbers for letters (A=1, B=2, C=3, etc.)

- Reverse the alphabet (A=Z, B=Y, C=X, etc.)
- Sliding scale alphabet (move the alphabet by one letter: A=B, B=C, C=D, etc.)
- Use invisible ink (write with lemon or lime juice; after it dries hold the paper up to a light source to read the message).
- Pigpen code: Each letter is represented by the part of the "pigpen" that surrounds it. If it's the second letter in the box, then it has a dot in the middle.

PIGPEN CODE

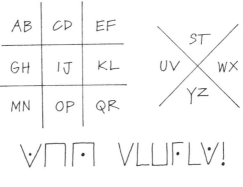

TOP SECRET!

YOUR SPY TEAM

The life of a spy can be a lonely one, with so much secrecy and subterfuge. It's much more fun to operate within a spy ring and work as a team to accomplish your undercover goals. On a team, spies can have specific tasks or areas of expertise, and of course code names.

The Agent-in-Charge: This is the head spy. She is responsible for directing, planning, and organizing the mission. All team members report to her.

The Scout: This is the person who scopes out the physical landscape to see if it's safe for the rest of the team to move in. She goes ahead of the team when they are out in the field, and no one moves in without a signal from her. She should have excellent eyesight and hearing and should be an expert on geography and the outdoors.

The Tracker: This person acts as the "trigger," the spy whose job it is to monitor the target of investigation. She tracks and observes the suspect's actions and alerts the rest of the team when the suspect is in range.

The Techie: This is the group's technology maven. She knows about computers, tools, and gadgets, from using them to fixing them to creating new ones. She is the one who draws up any maps, plans, or charts, and also keeps notes about the mission.

The Wheel Artist: This is the person who organizes the get-away, or who can use her wheels to accomplish any stealth maneuver. If she can drive, that's great, but she doesn't have to be commandeering a car. The wheels can be anything that gets your spy team out of the field in a timely manner. She can oversee a fleet of scooters, ride another spy to safety on her bike, or even accomplish a sensitive mission lightning-quick on her skateboard or roller skates.

The Stealth Master: This is a small, quiet person who can sneak into tight places and generally move around unnoticed. It helps if she is also a master of disguise, and an illusionist, able to use card and magic tricks for purposes of distraction.

The Social Engineer: This person is brave, chatty, outgoing, and able to interact with suspects and others to extract information. She can be the public face of the team while other team members gather evidence or perform surveillance, using her considerable social skills to both distract and engage.

After each mission, all members of the spy team should rendezvous at an agreed-upon meeting place or secret hideout, where they will report to the agent-in-charge and exchange information. No matter what her role on the team is, a spy should always note suspicious activity, try not to be seen or heard, cover her tracks, and never reveal her true identity to outsiders.

Coolest Paper Airplane Ever

Ordinary paper airplanes that look like jumbo jets and fighters are one thing. This airplane is something else altogether. We don't have an official name for it (why not make one up yourself?), but this folded wonder is something special.

HOW TO MAKE IT

A Take a piece of ordinary 8½″ × 11″ paper. Hold the paper so it's tall rather than wide, and fold the page in half lengthwise. Crease the center, using your fingernail. Unfold. That's fold #1.

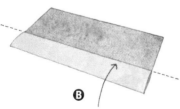

B Fold the left side in to touch the center crease. You've just made a new left edge. That's fold #2.

C Fold the new left edge to touch the center crease, creating again a new left edge (fold #3).

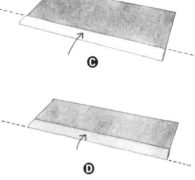

D Then fold the edge over the center line, and crease the top with your fingernail (fold #4).

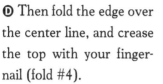

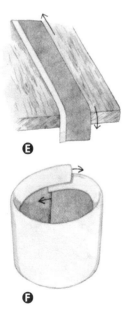

So you can make your airplane into a circle, soften the paper. Wrap it around your hand, or pull it against the edge of a desk or table, as when you curl ribbon **E**. This breaks down the fibers in the paper. Soon the paper will be very pliable, and you can bend it into a cylinder shape, with the folded edge on the inside. Slip one end of the fold under the other, about an inch or so, to hold everything in place **F**. Add tape to secure.

It looks like a squat tube, and the folded edge is the front of the plane **G**.

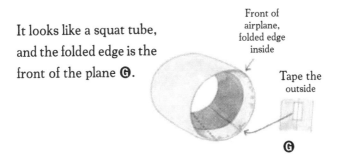

Front of airplane, folded edge inside

Tape the outside

G

HOW TO FLY IT

To fly, the plane needs power and spin. Hold it fully in your palm, facing forward. As you pull your arm back, ready to throw, flick your wrist and fingers. But, here's the trick: do not let your wrist or hand bend downward. Keep them straight up. This gives the plane spiral spin.

Be ready to use your determination and patience, as it may take some practice to perfect this technique. Once you have it down, though, your unique airplane will fly beautifully. And you'll use this same technique for tossing a football, so here you've learned two skills in one.

WHY IT WORKS

Airplanes—real and paper—stay in the air for two reasons. Understand these reasons, including a few technical terms, and you will possess the mental tools to design many a flying object.

Reason 1: The lift force is greater than the airplane's weight.

Lift is what keeps the plane up in the air. It happens when the air pressure pushing the plane up is more powerful than the pressure of air pushing the plane down. Lift counters the force of gravity, which always pulls objects back down to Earth.

Thrust

Lift

Gravity

Drag

Reason 2: The thrust force is stronger than drag.

Thrust gets the plane moving forward. In paper airplanes, thrust is the power of your toss. In real airplanes, designers keep materials as light as possible and use powerful engines. The heavier a plane is, the more thrust it needs.

Thrust counteracts drag, which is any quality that makes it harder to cut through the air (like sideways gravity). Here's a great way to explain drag: Turn your hand flat, palm down, and wave it back and forth, slicing the air horizontally. Then turn your hand sideways, thumb-up, pinkie-down, and wave it through the air, as if you are clapping or fanning yourself. Feel how much more air is in your way when your hand is sideways? That's drag. For airplanes, drag is the force of the air the plane must push through to get where it wants to go.

Airplanes fly when engines and wing design counter gravity and drag. Paper airplanes fly when you thrust them with gusto that overcomes gravity, and when they have a shape that is low-drag and can gracefully slice through the air. This creative design accomplishes everything you need to soar your new air flyer.

☙

Essential Gear

1. Swiss Army Knife

A key tool for survival, exploring, and camping, it's a knife, screwdriver, and saw with tons of extras like a magnifying glass, nail file, bottle opener, scissors, and tweezers. Best of all it fits in your pocket. Clean with hot soapy water, and add a tiny drop of mechanical oil once every three blue moons.

2. Bandana

Can be used to keep your head cool, protect your treasure, wrap a present. Tied to a stick, it can carry your treasured possessions on your adventures.

3. Rope and Twine

A stretch of rope and a knowledge of knots will take you many places—and may also help get you out of them.

4. Journal and Pencil, with a Back-up Pen

Life is about memories: a quick sketch of a bird or plant, a wishlist, a jot of the most important thought ever. A pad and pencil is also perfect for spying or for writing the Great American Novel.

5. Hair Band

For when hair gets in the way. In a pinch, you can also use your bandana, or a pencil.

6. Bungee Cord

For strapping things down on the go.

7. Flashlight

Basic tool for sleep outs and reading under the covers late at night. A small piece of red cellophane over the lens makes ghost stories even creepier. Eventually you can graduate to a headlamp, so your hands are free.

8. Compass

You need to know where you are, and a compass can help. Hang it around your neck along with a whistle.

9. Safety Pins

Because they're good to have on hand when things need to be put back together, or when you want to express eternal friendship to a new pal by decorating with a few beads as a gift.

10. Duct Tape
Two inches wide and hard as nails. It can fix almost everything. Good for clubhouse construction.

11. Deck of Cards and a Good Book
Old standbys.

12. Patience
It's a quality and not a thing, but it's essential so we'll include it here. Forget perfect on the first try. In the face of frustration, your best tool is a few deep breaths, and remembering that you can do anything once you've practiced two hundred times. Seriously.

Miscellanea

If you have yet to exhaust the possibilities of a languid summer's day, here are more things to do, in no particular order.

1. Skip Stones. Find a rock as smooth, flat, and round as possible. Hold it flattest-side down, index finger curled around one edge, and throw it sidearm, low and parallel to the water, snapping the wrist at the last possible moment before you let go to give it some spin. The stone should hit the water at a low, 20 degree angle or so. Keep practicing till the stone bounces off the water a few times.

2. Fly a Kite. Toss the kite into the wind, or run with the kite behind you until the wind catches it, then keeping the kite under control let the string out. If the kite swoops, pull on the string. Extra ribbons on the tail help to stabilize, and they are pretty too. Make sure there's enough wind, then practice so the string in your hand feels like second nature.

3. Throw Water Balloons. To fill, attach the mouth of the balloon to the water faucet (or use an adapter that comes with many packages of water balloons), and—this is key—keep the faucet on low so the water pressure doesn't send the balloon into outer space. Once the water balloon smashes to the ground, clean up the colorful scraps, since when the fun's over, the balloon remnants turn into trash.

4. Play Ping-Pong. Forget nudging your parents for a horse; ask for a ping-pong table instead. Have a good supply of those air-filled white balls ready for when they lodge in the crevices between storage boxes that have been stacked high against the basement walls to make space for the ping-pong table. If you're alone you can fold one of the table sides to vertical and push it against a wall to practice.

5. Play the Harmonica. Invaluable for nights by the campfire when the embers are low, the camp songs are over, and nearly everyone has fallen asleep. Hold the harmonica with your thumb and first finger. Blow breath into it, and draw it back through the holes. Experiment with sound. Flapping the other fingers up and down while you blow or draw will create a wavery vibrato.

6. Pop a Wheelie. Whether yours is a tough mountain bike or a ladylike pastel blue number with tassels out the handlebars and a basket, you'll want to know how to pop a wheelie. Once you're at speed, lean forward, hands grabbing the handlebars, and then shift your body weight slightly up and backward. That should be enough to lift the front wheel off the ground, whether you're doing show-offs on the street in front of your house, or trying to get your bike over tree stumps on a rugged trail.

7. Play Handball. Find a clean wall with no windows, or another flat surface, and bounce a pink rubber ball against it, open-handed. It's the best way possible to discover what your hands can do, and to learn about angles of reflection. Play alone or with friends, rotating in when someone misses the ball.

8. Take Things Apart. Old televisions and fax machines, a cell phone that no longer works, or a computer that's ten years out of date and living its final years in the back shed: no discarded machine should go undismantled. Teensy-tiny drivers and hex keys can unlock the smallest screws, so grab a hammer and whatever does the trick and see what's inside. That's how the world's best engineers learned what they know.

9. Make a Memory Box. This girlhood of yours is filled with days to remember. Make a scrapbook if you like, but really, any old box will do. Keep your mementos, letters, ticket stubs, the list of dreams scribbled on a napkin, a picture of your best friends, and the poem or phrase you thought up last night before bed. Stow this box of inspiration somewhere safe, keep adding to it, and don't look at it for twenty years.

10. Whittle. Put that Swiss Army knife to good use. With the knife in one hand and the wood in the other, shave off the bark and whittle away at fallen branches. No other directions are necessary; as you start trimming, the wood will begin to take shape, and you'll know when you're done. Keep the knife sharp (a whetstone comes in handy), and cut away from your body, hands and fingers, and away from anyone or thing that can get hurt.

11. Climb a Tree. Any tree. The trick is to push your legs and the plane of your body diagonally against the tree while your arms reach around the trunk. That way, you aren't trying to entirely defy gravity. Shimmy up the trunk this way inch by inch until you reach the branches, and then head for the sky.

12. Read Aloud. Summer afternoons are made for reading out loud to your family and friends. Sentences have rhythms that come alive with the sound of your voice. Act out the parts if you wish, or make up a play from the book's characters, or your own.

13. Go on a Scavenger Hunt. *Outdoors:* One person makes a list of things likely to be found in your backyard or local park. Then everyone else goes off on the hunt to find as many of those things as possible. The person who finds the most on her list wins! *Indoors:* Find items in the house beginning with each letter of the alphabet in order from A to Z. Or create a trail of clues to one ultimate "treasure" that your scavengers can discover.

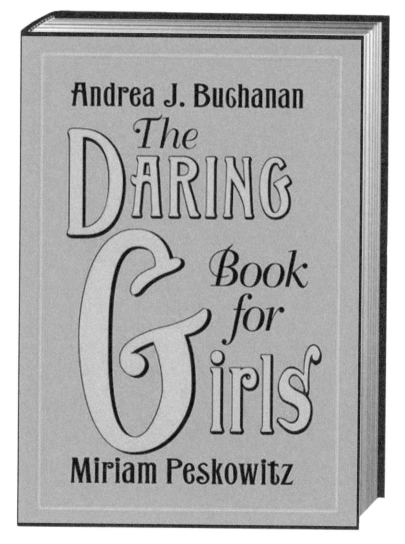

THE DARING BOOK FOR GIRLS

ISBN 978-0-06-147257-2 (hardcover)

*F*or every girl with an independent spirit and a nose for trouble, here is the original no-boys-allowed guide to everything from camping out to schoolyard games, to great women in history to the rules of Truth or Dare!

Inside You Will Find:

- How to Tie a Sari
- Olympic Female Athletes
- Hopscotch
- Building a Campfire
- Cootie Catchers
- Books That Will Change Your Life
- And much more!

Available wherever books are sold.

Collins *An Imprint of HarperCollinsPublishers*   www.harpercollins.com

The Pocket
DARING
Book
for
Girls

THINGS TO KNOW

Andrea J. Buchanan & Miriam Peskowitz

THE POCKET
DARING BOOK FOR GIRLS
Things to Know

ISBN 978-0-06-164994-3 (hardcover)

*T*his handy book brings together all the facts from the original *The Daring Book for Girls* (along with some tantalizing new ones)—fun and frivolous, entertaining and useful—into an easily portable guide. Whether it's queens of the ancient world, tide charts, or French phrases for any occasion, *The Pocket Daring Book for Girls: Things to Know* will make every girl and woman as clever as they have always wished to be!

Coming in November 2008

Available wherever books are sold.

Collins   *An Imprint of* HarperCollins*Publishers*   www.harpercollins.com

Daring Things I Have Done